BLOWING DOWN THE ROAD

DISCOVERING AMERICA'S DEEP SOUTH

TONY TINGLE

"Myth is such an integral part of the conception of the West. People think about it in terms of myth - always have."

Navarre Scott Momaday
- Writer and Storyteller

CONTENTS

Love to Amy, Carol, Ellie and Georgia who stayed at home but were with me every day. To Annie Pearl, Tom, Els, Carol, Joe, Mary, Boyd and Laurie, thanks for letting a stranger into your homes and your lives for a short while. Finally, thanks to Phil and Matt for making things happen.

INTRODUCTION

INTRODUCTION

As a youngster in the 1950s and 1960s I would go to watch the pictures at the Phoenix Cinema on Langsett Road, Sheffield, or (and this was something of a treat because it was further out of town and posher) the Hillsborough Park Cinema. Such neighbourhood cinemas have almost disappeared now but are still held fondly in the memory of the pre-video, pre-multiplex, pre-digital generation.

Regardless of any particular film's worth there was one cinematic device that never failed to captivate me; the transition from a night shot to a day shot. That moment at the end of a dimly-lit night scene when the screen would fade to black for a heartbeat and the next day would dawn bright and sunny on the screen. Just at that point of transition the small cinema would flood with light and I'd have to narrow my eyes ever so slightly to allow for the changed conditions. The shot could be a desert, the great plains or a small town waking up to a new morning. No matter; I was uplifted at such moments, entranced by the light and space on the screen.

Many of the films we would go to see were American and the association with light and space became set in stone in my imagination. America impressed me as a land of perpetual sunshine, the sky was always an unreasonable blue, the clouds tiny and unthreatening.

And what elbow room these Americans had! Movie characters travelled through limitless acres of space. Not just the Great South West of cowboy films either; even city suburbs gave room to breathe. All Americans seemed to live on broad handsome avenues with a front garden, large porch and white picket fence running round the house.

Light and space, that was the thing. That's what made an urban scruff trapped in a two-up, two-down terrace in the heavy industrial corridor of Sheffield's Don Valley gawp at the screen. Light and space. This was Hollywood of course, so the image of America being projected was, to say the very least, partial. The cinema left me ignorant of Pittsburgh's steel mills, Kentucky's coal mines and Detroit's car factories. I needed a few more years on my back before I worked out that someone had to claw Uncle Sam's promise out of the ground and forge it into someone else's wealth.

History quickened in 1960s America, modifying but deepening a growing infatuation. My anger and imagination was spurred more by events thousands of miles away than in my own back yard. People were visibly fighting for their futures over there. Political leaders and everyday heroes were being gunned down, fat sheriffs and dogs were loose in Selma and Birmingham till eventually the streets of Watts, Detroit and elsewhere caught fire.

I soaked up American writers for comfort and answers; Norman Mailer, James Baldwin, J.D Salinger, William Faulkner. They brought more comfort than answers.

The Grapes Of Wrath, George Jackson's prison experiences and Malcolm X's autobiography were suggestive but not definitive. Fuller answers were to come later in life. I've always been a bit slow to catch on.

And then there was the music. Born in 1950, I grew up with rock 'n' roll and was easy meat for the black American soul and R'n'B which white British 'beat' groups plagiarised, popularised and fed back to a receptive America.

For me Tamla and Atlantic records begat a love of Howlin' Wolf, Ray Charles, the blues, gospel and jazz. The close harmonies of The Beatles and The Beach Boys begat The Byrds who begat Gram Parsons, the Louvin Brothers and country music. Elvis Presley and Jerry Lee Lewis begat everything. Amen.

My musical heroes started me on a musical journey exploring the depths of American music at the same time as the civil rights movement roused my political allegiances. Whatever the starting point, all roads seemed to lead back to the Deep South.

This is where the idea of immersing myself in America began to germinate, but the seed never took root. I could tell you that marriage, children and the need to earn a living snuck up on me, but the truth is that at 20 years of age I didn't have the imagination or single-mindedness to roll the dice. Forty years later retirement and the confidence of having negotiated my way through adulthood - sometimes well, sometimes badly - combined with the limitless reach of the internet to bring America back into focus. Our kitchen table began to fill up with maps, travel writing and scribbled notes, out of which emerged a plan to journey from New York, down the eastern seaboard to Georgia, due west through the Deep South and then the mythic lands of the Great South West to California, the Pacific Coast Highway and San Francisco. The plan was commendably detailed at the start of the journey, shading towards worryingly vague at the end, but it was a plan all the same.

Weeks later I was sat nervously, fingers hovering over the computer keyboard. I stood up, paced around the back room, returned to the computer. The webpage on the screen showed I was about to book a one-way flight to New York. If I pressed the 'Enter' key it would happen. I took a deep breath, pressed the key, stretched, put my hands on my head and whispered "Jesus Christ!".

THE JOURNEY

LEAVING

I'd been greedy - 90 days is the maximum length of time allowed on a visitor's visa to the USA and I'd planned to use up almost all of it on my journey. What had seemed so obviously a good idea at the planning stage curled at the edges when the actuality hit and I had to say my goodbyes. No looking back as I left family and comfortable everyday certainties outside the airport. No looking back on the walk into the terminal. This was going to be much harder for those who cared about me but were staying at home; my greed for America had brought doubt and guilt along for the ride, so definitely no looking back.

THE CROSSING

The first clue that I was visiting a country with which we share a common language but a divergent culture was contained in the airline's shopping magazine, 'Sky Mall'. I'd never before seen an airline magazine advertising 'Litter Kwitter', an item of furniture handily doubling as a toilet for domestic cats who might be unfamiliar with the great outdoors. This blind spot may have marked me as a relatively unsophisticated traveller but how about the zombie garden ornament, designed to rise from the dead out of your carefully manicured lawn, or the lifesize Yeti home ornament for that uninhabited corner of the living room? I admit I was intrigued. Not so much by the goods themselves, more by wondering how the lucky purchaser would get them off the plane.

If the attentive service of the airline staff was a harbinger of the American service industry's obsession with the 'customer experience', the customs guard at JFK airport was a worrying reminder of the US state's steely core. This one man, on his own judgement, could refuse me entry to the United States with no possibility of appeal. If any doubt crept into his mind about me, I would simply be turned around and put on the next flight home.

All smiles on first greeting, the customs man's eyes narrowed when I told him I planned to roam around his country without a chaperone for three months. A string of questions followed about where I was going, who I was staying with and what I was going to do. It felt like a wrong step could put an end to my plans there and then, but I suspect my age and unambiguously pale complexion counted in my favour with the guard. I was waved through - the continent of my teenage dreams was mine to explore.

NEW YORK
EPISODES

NEW YORK EPISODES

Visiting a city as huge as New York for just a few days both the good things that happen, as well as the bad, are usually pure dumb luck of one kind or another.

Walking up Broadway and stumbling across Greenwich Village; sitting in Union Square (the traditional gathering place for the left and the labour movement to protest) in spring sunshine; walking through affluent, beautiful Central Park outpacing perfectly attired but snail-slow joggers; the view from the overground section of the J train crossing the Hudson river via Williamsburg bridge; jerk chicken, boiled cabbage, green beans and a small half-and-half in the Bed-Stuy Fish Fry cafe ("$10 sir, thank you and have a nice day"); a mid-week, afternoon Yankees game and listening to knowledgeable, die-hard fans trading game statistics on the subway coming back; the surprisingly elegant architecture of some of the low-rise buildings hemmed in by their giant neighbours – all joyful experiences.

My lodgings were in Brooklyn or, more precisely, Bedford-Stuyvesant, which is a working class predominantly black neighbourhood. Given the degree of informal segregation that exists in the States, 'predominantly' means 'overwhelmingly'. I don't mind admitting that I felt anxious being out on the street there at first. My anxiety wasn't based on anything that happened to me; nobody did or said anything remotely threatening the whole time I was there. I got a few sideways glances as I passed but then again everything about me would have screamed 'different' in Bedford-Stuyvesant.

On my first walk round the neighbourhood my ignorance (I'm using the word in its literal sense – I knew as little of this world as the people here did of mine) played on my fears. It was a Sunday afternoon, everyone was out on the street, including knots of youngsters. 'Sore thumb' doesn't do justice to how conspicuously alien I felt. Two armed, plain-clothed cops were openly rousting a young black lad as I passed by.

There's a cop station right in the middle of Bedford-Stuyvesant and the cops do a thing where they drive, very slowly, through the streets in the early hours with their sirens going at about half-power, I think it must be just to keep everyone on their toes and let them know they're around. They woke me up a couple of times doing this.

As luck would have it my hunger out-fought my anxiety on that first walk round and led me to the Bed-Stuy Fish Fry fast food place and a memorable hour eating their remarkable jerk chicken and watching the working people who keep New York going come in to collect their takeaway meals, greet their neighbours, shoot the breeze and leave. These were people just keeping their heads above water if they stood on tiptoe.

By the end of my stay I'd grown comfortable enough to go in the local barbers for a full cut-throat shave; head and face. Best shave I've ever had. The tall lugubrious barber who did me wasn't very talkative, but in response to an item on the news (the TV is on everywhere in New York) he asked me if I thought there was more cancer around these days 'because of all the shit that's around'. I said I thought maybe it's just that there's more awareness of it these days, at which he nodded his head. I took this to mean he would take my suggestion into consideration. At the end of the shave he looked at me and said, 'You clean, boy'.

It was six short blocks to walk from my digs to the Gates Avenue subway station. In those six blocks I noted the following store-front churches; The Mission For Christ Right Way Pentecostal Church, The Healing Deliverance Church, The House Of Prayer, The Pentecostal Hope Of God, The Pilgrim Church, The African Episcopal Methodist Church and, my favourite, The Faith Assemblies Of God Inc. I love the Inc. The people of Bedford-Stuyvesant may be downtrodden but damn it they're given every opportunity to be saved.

A sign on a front door on the way to the station reads, "Obama – History Made". The sign looks old now and a little tattered.

I got hauled into a rather one-way conversation with an old black guy in a diner near the Rockefeller Centre. It started when a reference was made to Obama on the TV; "Obama, Obama", he sneered, a dismissive wave of the hand. "He ain't the President, someone else the President". I think this is pretty insightful and tell him so in so many words. This encourages him to go further. "Nixon, he was the man, only President I made money under". My heart sinks but he goes on to clarify, "Everybody was on the make under Nixon" he confides, and cackles. After a little more talk he leaves, imparting a little more New York wisdom "Hold on to what you got boy. Hold on to what you got".

My host in Bedford-Stuyvesant was Lazarus. In conversation he tells me that he speaks Spanish and Portuguese which he learnt 'en las calles' (in the streets). Lazarus manages a number of properties, including the one I was in, for his uncle's property development company. He looks like a young Frank Zappa, which endeared me to him for a while. Lazarus works long hours, probably most of it legally, though while I'm there he spends a lot of time 'en las calles' – underneath my window in fact – shifting scrap metal with his mates.

Lazarus is discontented and wants to get out and run a farm; his plan is to raise the grain locally that is currently transported thousands of miles cross-country to make beer sold in New York. His wife is in New Jersey raising chickens and growing vegetables. He says there's plenty of land to farm in New Jersey still and thinks they can make a go of it. I think of the impossibility of making this come true; of the vast

DIVOR

Pl
Spouse's Sig

DIVORC
1-800

Se H
www.TheDiv

CE $399

urt Fee
re NOT Needed

CENTER™

14-0333

Español

ceCenter.com

DIVORCE, NEW YORK STYLE

amounts of capital and the contacts needed, the officials to be bribed and the vested interests who would make sure it didn't happen, one way or another. I've heard or read somewhere that everybody in New York has a story to tell and every New Yorker has a dream. This is Lazarus's dream.

Lazarus is also a hustler; he tries to hustle me at the end of my stay and because I won't play ball I'm left at the last minute without a ride to Penn Station to catch my train to Savannah. But, no matter, he's a small-time hustler in a city of big-time hustlers.

I saw the big-time hustlers close up, though I hadn't meant to. It happened when I visited the Natural History Museum, which borders the west side of Central Park. I loved the place and had to be thrown out at 5.30pm. Did you know that around 10,000 years ago North America still contained pygmy camels and ant eaters the size of grizzly bears? Their bones have been faithfully reassembled and are on display in the museum. I can't get enough of this stuff but having been ejected there's nothing for it but to stroll across the park over to the east side. Skyscrapers form the backdrop to the trees on three sides and as you near the main east side exit the path slopes downwards quite sharply. The further down the path you progress the more the monstrous scale of these buildings in front of you becomes apparent. There's some kind of optical illusion such that when you're directly underneath they almost seem to bend over and stare down at you.

I was totally unprepared – this is the Waldorf-Astoria, Trump Tower, the Apple building and more opulence in one place than you'd care to see in a lifetime.

It's pedestrian rush hour on the Upper East side, but unlike the other bits of the city I'd walked through Upper East side-ers weren't making a bee-line for the subway. Liveried doormen were whistling for taxis for well-heeled hotel guests. Others, equally well-heeled, had the anticipatory look of someone making for happy hour at the singles bar.

I know for sure they're not making for the subway station because it's in the opposite direction to which everyone, except me, seems to be headed. As I'm being trampled on by these posh New Yorkers I visualise the scene in the film 'Billy Liar' where Tom Courtenay imagines mowing down family and friends with a machine-gun, but the moment passes. Later, from the top of the Rockefeller Centre, these skyscrapers look beautiful - like a dreamscape - but it's impossible for me to look at them without being angered at the colossal concentration of wealth, power and privilege they represent.

Dumb luck came to my rescue when I went to see the New York Yankees baseball team. The Yankees are to baseball what Manchester United are to football and as they were in town at the same time as me I felt I had to go and see them, especially as the cheap seats were only $5. I made my way there full of anticipation on a rainy Wednesday evening until a puzzled looking steward pointed out that my on-line ticket was in fact for the following night (baseball teams play almost every day in the summer – 160+ games a season). I'm sure the word 'schmuck' would have formed in the steward's mind even if customer service etiquette prevented him from saying it out loud. I left Yankee Stadium abashed and returned the following night hoping I wouldn't run into the same steward. The Wednesday night game had been abandoned due to the rain but the Thursday game went ahead as planned; dumb luck conquers dumb organisation.

Major league baseball is a great show. Pitchers can throw the ball at close on 100 mph, batters hit the ball impossible distances. Even mishits (called, euphemistically, 'pop-ups') fly way higher than a cathedral spire. Yankee fans are worth watching too. They dish out approval and disapproval in equal measure and at equal volume. I loved every minute of it even though my seat was so high up I had to take a lift to get to it.

The Yankees won. At the end of the game their beloved veteran pitcher, Mariano Rivera, walked out from the bull pen (where the pitchers warm up) to finish off the opposition of the day, the Minnesota Twins.

To Yankee fans, Rivera is what Bobby Charlton was to Manchester United, or Bobby Moore, Geoff Hurst and Martin Peters to West Ham. As he walks out the public address system plays 'Enter Sandman' by Metallica at full volume and the crowd goes crazy, singing along ('Say your prayers little one, sleep with one eye open......'). This is a warning to the batter who tries to look nonchalant but has 30,000 people baying for his blood and one of the best closing pitchers who ever lived just 60 feet away. Mariano duly puts the last 3 batters to sleep in 7 pitches, Frank Sinatra sings 'New York' ('If I can make it there I'll make it anywhere'...), the crowd sing along and we all pile out on to the subway.

> *On my way to the station at 4.00am in the morning walking through Bedford-Stuyvesant, a woman approaches me for money. 'Could you give me 50 cents for a bag of chips (crisps) sir.' I rummage around in my pocket for some change and put some in her hand, It's pitch-black at this hour but within an instant, and I mean an instant, the woman says 'That's 5 cents short sir'.*

NEW YORK TO SAVANNAH

The train to Savannah pulled out of Penn Station just about on time. I'd arrived at the station more than an hour and a half early, about 4.30am. Street people had also chosen this time, when security was much less visible than last time I'd visited the station, to make their early morning rounds of the litter baskets.

New York to Savannah is about 800 miles, a 14 hour train journey. Amtrak gives names to their trains; Texas Eagle, Pacific Surfliner, Heartland Flyer, City Of New Orleans ("Good morning America, how are you…."). The New York to Savannah train is the Palmetto 89.

There's a reminder that we're off to the eastern end of the bible belt; the train guard punching my ticket fixes me squarely in the eye and says "God bless you". Every passenger gets the same blessing. The conviction behind the words is well-meant and well-received, though the blessing itself is unfortunately lost on an atheist.

South of New York, through New Jersey and Delaware, our train travels through a heavily industrial landscape. Much of it is post-industrial these days though; hulks of factories, warehouses and stockyards stand abandoned, and look as if they've been that way for some time. America may still be a military superpower, but it isn't the industrial powerhouse it once was, and we're rolling past some of the evidence.

As we move into Maryland the land shakes off the grip of industry. For the next 700 or so miles Palmetto 89 carries us through the fertile coastal plain, small lakes and wetlands, meadows, homestead-style clapboard houses and small low-rise (rarely more than 2-storey) towns. The houses show some slight variations on a theme; red brick covers the lower third of some, styles of porches and frontages vary. Most stand in many acres of land and most porches contain at least one rocking chair. As we get further south and the temperature starts to climb, more and more of the porch rocking chairs are occupied.

It seems remarkable that the America that is most strongly implanted in the mind from the cinema is the one that's rolling past us for mile after mile.

Passing through Washington DC we catch a glimpse of the White House dome off to the right of the train. Through the middle states of Virginia and North Carolina the seasons start to change. The oak, pine and redwood trees which were bare in New York begin to sprout leaves. A thin row of trees accompanies the tracks virtually all the way down and by the time we reach our destination they're in full bloom.

I can pinpoint where I see my first Confederate flag; it's planted outside a house bordering the tracks between the towns of Selma and Wilson in South Carolina. The flag seems to go unnoticed by the group of ersatz union soldiers behind us who are on their way to a civil war re-enactment in Charleston being held to mark the

150th anniversary of the start of the war. Two of the group are wearing reproduction union army uniform, which stirs some interest when they first get on the train.

As the young student sat next to me is deep into her laptop and iPod and not encouraging conversation I'm forced by circumstance to listen in on this group's conversation for long stretches of time.

The re-enactment will last something like a week, they will be under canvas during that time and strict adherence to army discipline and seniority will have to be observed. The self-appointed leader has clearly never allowed himself the luxury of an unexpressed thought in his life. He's a sergeant in this fictitious army and he's a veteran at these events. He expounds at length to the rest of the group, some of whom are re-enactment virgins, on how things will work during the week.

Tension mounts when one of the enthusiastic newcomers asks if he can recruit some of his other friends for the next re-enactment. This doesn't go down well with the veteran who makes it clear that they themselves are only there on trial – "No offence, but you guys aren't my 'A' team" – having only had a weekend's training themselves. It appears that the honour of the regiment is at stake and duties will have to be carried out meticulously during the week.

After a while the discussion revolves around the possibility of the newcomers playing a part in firing one of the big guns, but again the door is firmly shut in the faces of the rookies; "I'll be relying on the more seasoned people for the artillery rounds," explains el supremo. Besides which, it seems that one of the newcomers is slightly deaf, raising serious questions in the sergeant's mind about whether he'd be able to hear the order to fire.

The belligerents, along with most of the other passengers, get off at Charleston, leaving just a handful of us to complete the journey to Savannah. As we leave them behind it occurs to me that there's potential for disharmony, perhaps even mutiny, after a few drinks and some uncomfortable nights under canvas, leaving open the possibility that the Confederacy have a fighting chance of winning this time round.

The heat is heavy in Savannah and I find out later that the weather has been unusually hot for early April; it's been in the 90s and will stay that way for most of my stay. I learn this from Burke, my taxi driver who has an engagingly lazy drawl compared to the fast-talking New Yorkers. He hangs on to every word like it's a precious commodity and in my head I'm finishing his sentences for him. Burke, and this turns out to be the pattern with many Americans I get into conversation with, works six days a week, 10-12 hours a day. Through the overtaking mirror I can see Burke's eyes half-closed on occasion followed by a quick adjustment on the steering wheel to get us back on line. He gets me safely to my lodgings, however, and leaves me his phone number in case I want to book him for the journey out of Savannah. I promise I'll give him first refusal and mean it – I love the sound of his voice and hope to hear it again.

SAVANNAH

Savannah is picture-postcard pretty, or at least the Landmark Historic District is. My lodgings were on the edge of the Historic District and if there's an 'other side of the tracks' district, and there usually is, I didn't get to see it. Savannah is regularly cited as one of the most beautiful cities in the country; if you wanted to shoot a re-make of 'Gone With The Wind', this place would be on your short list.

The city, which sits on the Savannah river, was first settled by colonialists in the mid-18th Century, although native Americans - the Yamacraws - beat Europeans to the spot by a long stretch. The intriguing thing about the Historic District is that it is laid out in a series of 24 squares which are now shady, tree-lined resting places but were originally planned as mustering centres for the local militia at times of military threat. Savannah was established as a first line of defence for the prospering cities to the north against the Spanish who were encamped in Florida. In time, cotton and the city's strategic transport position on the Savannah river made the city (or at least some of it) rich in its own right.

My first afternoon is spent in the Charles H. Morris Memorial Centre. I had been lucky enough to time my visit with the final day of Savannah's annual music festival and got a ticket to see 'The Infamous Stringdusters', an up-and-coming country/bluegrass band. I'm familiar with some of their music and I'm keeping my fingers crossed. Some of their studio recordings can be a bit pedestrian and I'm hoping I've not wasted my money.

In fact they're a revelation on stage. Six relatively young musicians from Virginia, the Stringdusters pull off the trick of finding new ways to play traditional music. Each inventive solo on dobro, fiddle or mandolin is followed by a burst of applause with some adventurous souls even attempting a square-dance in very limited space. The Savannah crowd may be solidly middle-aged but they're genuinely receptive to the youngsters' old-time music. The skill of the band, the enthusiasm of the crowd and their shared love of the music make my first concert in America a memorable one.

Country music is pretty much an acquired taste - and very much a minority interest - outside the USA. The association with big hats, maudlin lyrics ("When you leave, walk out the door backwards so it looks like you're comin' home...."), religiosity ("Drop-kick me Jesus through the goalposts of life...") and reactionary politics is unfortunate. But at its best country music can move you as surely as the blues and it has shown a remarkable ability to re-invent and re-invigorate itself. It did it in the late 60s/early 70s, again with the 'alternative' country movement, and the Stringdusters, and others, are carrying the torch for a new generation.

The following day I take a walk down by the riverfront area, which has been redeveloped specifically to cater for the tourist industry. If you can imagine an upmarket, sub-tropical Bridlington harbour with paddle steamers you've just about got it. And give your imagination a pat on the back.

On my way back from the riverfront area I'm a bit surprised to see street signs next to a number of parking bays which read, rather ominously, "Reserved For The FBI". That doesn't seem very security-conscious to me. I want to take a photograph to prove I've not made it up. But what if it's a kind of honey-trap for tourists with terrorist sympathies? I imagine FBI agents steaming out of the building the instant I take my camera out. Another sucker snagged. I probably arouse more suspicion by passing the same spot two or three times going in different directions but I eventually shake off my timidity, get the shot, and scurry off expecting a firm tap on the shoulder all the way back to my lodgings.

My host in Savannah is Rick, an ex-international banker who couldn't stand the financial rat-race any more and used the stash he made from banking to buy property in the Savannah area. He rents his properties out, mainly to students at the Savannah College of Art & Design, and lives off the proceeds. He's a good host and we get on OK. We dance around the politics a little bit; Rick thinks America should not be involved in Libya, but because he thinks the government needs to sort out their budget crisis and balance the books rather than on any principled grounds. Once a banker.....

The royal wedding is all over the press in the States and Rick is keen to know what the English, as represented by me, think of it. A chill enters the room when I tell him that my youngest daughter Georgia was proudly wearing a 'Stuff The Wedding' badge to school when I left the country. In for a penny, in for a pound I think, so I start to dig up as much dirt on the royals as my memory can handle: Harry (or was it William?) dressing as a Nazi; Andrew consorting with a convicted paedophile who also happens to be a multi-millionaire; Sarah Ferguson's repeated financial scandals. I should have hit him with Prince Charles wanting to be a tampax too, but it slips my mind at the time.

Rick gets my first Henderson's Relish award. I've brought over three bottles of Henderson's Relish which I will award to people who've helped to make my stay over here enjoyable, and I think he qualifies. I explain during the presentation ceremony that we put the relish on stews and pies in the long dark English winters. Rick doesn't exactly run round the house holding the bottle above his head in triumph but I reckon he's quietly impressed.

On Sunday afternoon I take a walk through Forsyth Park which is the centrepiece of the Historic District. A simple, elegant monument has the inscription "To The Confederate Dead 1861 – 1865" and I wonder what the many black people who pass by this monument every day think of it. There are war monuments all over Savannah. 'History' in this city seems to be an abbreviation for military history. There's even a memorial to the heroes of a war I've never heard of – the Anglo-Spanish war of 1779, part of the American Revolutionary War, in which Savannah came under siege.

I'm frustrated by my ignorance of the natural world while I'm here. There's just so much of it – nature, that is – all around, encouraged by the sub-tropical climate, and I don't know any of it. I'm sure the flowers must include azaleas, I can just about recognise a pine tree now and an oak, but that's about it. I go on a historical architectural tour which turns out to be very informative (the alternative was a ghost tour) and learn what Spanish moss looks like. Some progress.

But the birdsong is completely new to me, I've never heard anything like it. I sit in the squares and listen to the birds at length but have no idea which bird is making which call. If there are any experts in the field reading this, there are a few bird songs I've been hearing all over the south that I need help with. One sounds like a high-pitched 'Sugar babe, sugar babe, sugar babe', another one goes 'Hurdy gurdy, hurdy gurdy, hurdy gurdy' and another one goes 'Whoop, whoop, whoop', starting quite softly and getting progressively louder and faster. Any help from ornithologists specialising in birds of the southern states of America would be very welcome.

On leaving day I rang Burke, whose answer phone message ended "God bless you and keep you." He returned my call and we arranged for him to pick me up and take me to Savannah airport, where there would be a hire car waiting for me. I told Burke I was going to Macon, Georgia, using the old Highway 80 route, as I'd read that it's very scenic. Burke's professional sensibilities were outraged. "Gonna take you forever," he advised and strongly suggested that I take the interstate highway. It was the most animated I'd seen him by some distance so I felt I had to take his views on the matter seriously. After thinking it over, and since it was already mid-afternoon and I didn't want to be on the road after dark on my first day of driving in America, I told Burke that I was going to follow his advice.

In the taxi I was paying close attention to traffic conditions as I would be negotiating them shortly. After about 10 minutes I realised that I'd not seen a single traffic roundabout while I'd been in the States and I told Burke this. "What the hell's a roundabout?" he asked. I had a stab at explaining in a couple of sentences but I don't think I got the concept over and gave up. You try explaining a traffic roundabout to someone who's never seen one, it's not easy.

NATCHEZ TRACE OLD ROAD, MISSISSIPPI

SAVANNAH TO
WARM SPRINGS

I looked at the hire car with some misgivings. I was excited about long-distance driving, though the thought of negotiating the big cities was daunting. It was more the prospect of handling an automatic for the first time. It had been impossible to hire a manual drive so I was stuck with it, but my imagination toyed with the scenario of looking around in the footwell for an absent gear lever rather than following the white line on the road and the unfortunate consequences that might bring. Nonetheless, after a brief familiarisation session – four or five times round the car park – I set off down the airport road on to the I-16 bound for Macon.

This was still flatland, and was to remain so until I reached the western edge of Georgia a couple of days later; that's about 300 miles with nothing remotely resembling so much as a sharp incline. Taking into account the 800 miles I'd travelled south on roughly the same terrain the coastal plain was taking on impressive proportions and I was starting to get a feel for the scale of the country. Driving due west, with the sun starting to sink in the sky directly in front of me, it felt like this was a large part of what I'd come for – movement, light and space.

I suppose I must share that bit of the 'American dream' which is about having the freedom to go where the mood takes you, a chance to properly breathe. It's a dream, like the rest of the American dream, which is denied to most Americans most of the time. Many towns, and some big cities, don't even have a viable public transport system, as I was to find out later in the trip.

Part of my first day on the road was spent at the Georgia Music Hall Of Fame in Macon. Georgia has a good claim to host a music hall of fame and Macon has an excellent claim on being the venue. Little Richard was born in Macon. Ray Charles, who with Sam Cooke was the first artist to secularise gospel music and harness it to an R&B shuffle to make soul music, came from nearby Albany. Otis Redding, the artist who arguably more than any other popularised soul music, lived in Macon from being a youngster. Other lesser known figures in country, blues, jazz and rock music (Blind Willie McTell, Gram Parsons, Fletcher Henderson, The Allman Brothers Band) have strong Georgia connections.

The Hall Of Fame is a worthy effort but at the time of my visit I'm the only one there (this will become a bit of a theme) and I wonder how long it will last. The very helpful woman on reception had told me that the entrance fee also covered admission to the graves of two of the Allman Brothers Band but much as I love music, and much as I love their music particularly, I'd decided to draw the line at worshipping at their graveside.

From the Hall Of Fame I drove over the Otis Redding bridge to the Ocmulgee national monument. In researching the trip I'd been surprised at the number of native American sites that have been preserved. Ocmulgee is one of them. The Creek, or Muscogee, people settled at the Ocmulgee site from about 900AD, established a stockaded township of log dwellings. The Creek were expert farmers and built a number of earthwork mounds, probably for political and religious purposes. The 50 feet-high mounds don't look much at first sight but become much more impressive when you learn that they contained internal structures requiring complex engineering skills and had to be built by thousands of individuals moving earth manually using only small baskets.

On a warm sunny day it's a peaceful walk along the mile-long plateau which runs between the mounds. This would have been the site of the main Muscogee township site and walking along in complete silence, apart from the breeze, and with a panoramic view of the lush Georgia countryside to enjoy it's not hard to understand why this spot was chosen.

The Muscogee settled this land for centuries but their peace was broken, first by the Spanish who brought diseases to which the native Americans had no immunity, then by the English who traded with them for a while but then went to war when the natives objected to being swindled in the trading of fur, and finally by the American government who wanted the land and in the 1830s moved the whole nation 1200 miles to Oklahoma in the Muscogees' own 'Trail of Tears'. When the railroad came through a few years afterwards the township and a large part of one of the sacred mounds was destroyed.

Leaving Macon I moved on to Warm Springs, a small town established in beautiful wooded countryside on the edge of the FDR National Park. Warm Springs is a tiny place (one road in, one road out) on the Georgia-Alabama border. I stayed in the enticingly named 'Meriwether Inn', where stagecoaches used to stop before the internal combustion engine. You can almost smell blueberry pie cooling on the window sills here.

There is farmland all around, and I passed iconic trucks (huge gleaming radiator grills, smokestacks either side of the driver's cabin, oversize overtaking mirrors, the whole bit) shifting impressive amounts of timber further down the hill, but the main function of Warm Springs these days seems to be to prise open the wallets of tourists visiting the 'Little White House' up the road. The Little White House was the summer retreat of the 32nd President of the United States, Franklin Delano Roosevelt, who visited here in the hope of finding relief from the polio which struck him early in life. He liked the area so well he bought up a fair chunk of it and the house is now a national museum.

I'd planned a walk in the pine forests of FDR National Park, which was my main purpose in coming to this part of Georgia. Unaccountably, despite the fact that my destination was only a couple of miles away, and it's a sizeable National Park, I got lost on the way. I called in at a petrol station and was pleased to see a grizzled old-timer at the counter so I was confident he'd be able to direct me. He pointed me in the right direction but as I was walking out the door he looked up from his newspaper and growled "Look out for the rattlesnakes." I looked back for a sign of reassurance that this was the old-timer's idea of a joke but he'd already gone back to reading his newspaper.

I'm an occasional countryside walker rather than an a committed hiker. When I set off on a walk it's generally in the back of my mind that every step I take away from my launch point is an additional one I'm going to have to take coming back and this can put a dampener on the occasion for me. But this walk was a dream for the uncommitted rambler. It was only about 4.5 miles long, shaded by pine trees all the way round and with a small creek for company for most of the journey. For the first mile or so the going was eased even further by a thick covering of pine needles, like walking on a shag pile carpet. This is my kind of hiking.

> *In my first couple of weeks since coming south I've been hearing the train whistle everywhere. And I mean everywhere; in my room in Savannah, at the motel in Macon, driving on the I-16. I hear it now in this Georgia pine forest in the middle of a national park. It's not really a whistle, more of a moan, like an animal in pain. It's an incredibly evocative noise, redolent of place, which would explain why there have been so many songs written about it ("I'll never see that gal of mine, Lord I'm in Georgia doin' time, I heard that lonesome whistle blow") and why it works its way into so many films about the South.*

As I returned to base camp from my walk I noticed a sign that I should have paid more attention to on the way out. It says that there has been an unusual number of rattlesnake sightings recently and walkers need to exercise vigilance. The old-timer wasn't pulling my leg.

I paid a visit to the 'Little White House' before leaving Warm Springs. It's surprisingly modest – living/dining room, bedroom, kitchen, secretary's bedroom and pantry and that's it. The servants had to be content with sharing a two-storey garage with FDR's car.

The Little White House museum tells Roosevelt's life story, with an understandable emphasis on the times he spent in Warm Springs, and the fact that he died in this house while he was having his portrait painted. The museum claims that his familiarity with the problems being faced by poor farmers he met in Warm Springs helped to shape some of Roosevelt's New Deal policies for agriculture.

The displays make me think about the bile towards Obama that's been spewing out of the media while I've been here; mainly, but not wholly, via the Fox Channel. Roosevelt is now a revered figure, yet he was 'big government' personified, using federal funding and state intervention on an unprecedented scale to try to pull the system out of the deepest depression it had faced up to then. Roosevelt was anything but a socialist, he came from an extremely privileged background, was a fully paid up member of the American ruling class and played a key part in reining in the growing militancy of American workers in the 1930s, but compared to Obama this now much-revered figure looks like a Bolshevik. This is the extent to which free market, neo-liberal ideas now dominate ruling circles in the USA and beyond.

I'm becoming accustomed to driving the automatic now, though my left (clutch) foot is very much underused compared to when I'm driving at home. I'm wondering whether I could employ it to do something useful on the longer drives, like learning how to sketch with it, or shell peanuts.

Later in the day I travelled further west, across the Chattahoochee river, into a different state, Alabama, and a different time zone.

MONTGOMERY

That's not quite it for Georgia. I hesitate to tell the story but it's good to get things off your chest I think. When I was driving through the FDR National Park I'd seen a sign showing a scenic drive to a place called 'Dowdell's Knob'. The infant in me couldn't resist being able to say that I'd stood on Dowdell's Knob and admired the view. So I did. On the morning I left Warm Springs. And the view is spectacular...

If the Georgia countryside had been remarkably well-manicured (as if some grateful god mowed the Georgia grass every morning in return for the Georgians' devotions) on first view Alabama seemed noticeably more rough-hewn.

Arrival in Montgomery was fraught. It's surrounded on three sides by freeway and although I'd booked my accommodation ahead, internet directions to the motel were vague. I took a wrong turn, and when you go wrong on one of these urban freeways you go wrong in a big way. That episode, and an evening cooped up in my motel room afraid to join the thundering traffic on the freeway outside my door, convinced me that I'd see little of America other than motel rooms without a GPS.

Thanks to Walmart I acquired a new travelling companion the following morning. She (the GPS has a woman's voice) is a little sharp in giving directions I find, and occasionally sounds impatient with me, especially if I misinterpret her directions. This happens quite often in our first few journeys together. I christen her Henrietta as her voice puts me in mind of the hen of the same name in the Foghorn Leghorn cartoons.

I went to visit the Civil Rights Memorial in downtown Montgomery. A simple and sombre place constructed in memory of those people who were murdered by cops or racists during the civil rights struggle. There is little of an explanatory nature here but that's not its purpose. Each person remembered has a plaque with a brief biography and account of how they died.

The stories of some of those remembered here will be known to many – Medgar Evers, Emmett Till, the three 'Freedom Riders' whose murders were portrayed in the film 'Mississippi Burning' – but I'm taken by the lesser known stories and the courage they represent. William Lewis Moore, for example, a white Baltimore postal worker and CORE (Congress of Racial Equality) activist who undertook to walk alone across the Deep South to deliver a letter calling for racial tolerance to the Governor of Mississippi. Moore was shot and killed as he rested by the roadside in Alabama. Herbert Lee, a black Mississippi farmer led a campaign to register black voters in his district – a very dangerous business – who was shot in broad daylight by a state legislator. Lee's body lay untouched for hours before anyone dared to collect it. His murderer was never arrested. The vast majority of the 41 murder cases highlighted by the Memorial remain 'unsolved'.

The Memorial has a 'Wall of Tolerance', which is a video screen about 30 feet wide by 15 feet high; it takes up the whole of one wall in a sizeable room. Names imprinted digitally on the screen drift slowly downwards, echoing the water feature by the memorial's entrance. These are the names of people who have visited the memorial and pledged to take a stand against hatred and to work for tolerance.

I take an invitation to add my name and catch my breath as it appears in the middle of the screen and then finds its place with the half a million others rolling down the screen. It was only a symbolic gesture but an emotionally powerful one all the same, one that will stay with me and that I'll try to live up to.

The memorial was established under the umbrella of the Southern Poverty Law Centre, an organisation I'd come across researching the trip. I'd been intrigued that such an organisation should be based in Alabama and emailed them from home to ask if I could interview someone about SPLC's purpose and history. They'd agreed in principle but we'd not been able to fix a date and time. As the centre was right across the street from the memorial, I decided to push my luck and ask if someone would be prepared to talk to me that afternoon. It worked, and I got to spend an hour talking with Penny Weaver, SPLC's Communications Coordinator.

I'd assumed from SPLC's name that it was a welfare rights organisation, but that's not really the case. As it was explained to me, 'poverty law' is a body of laws, legal regulations and precedents that poor people in the USA can use to address issues that affect them in their day-to-day lives. The SPLC was established in the early 1970s. Its aim was to use the poverty law to address issues of discrimination. The organisation established its reputation by fighting and winning cases on behalf of women being excluded from law enforcement jobs. In the 1970s there were still no black Alabama state troopers until the SPLC successfully brought a case on behalf of Philip Paradise, a black man who wanted to join the force. Opposition was intense; for a while Alabaman authorities stopped recruiting state troopers altogether rather than recruit blacks.

Since the 1980s the SPLC has concerned itself increasingly with taking civil actions on behalf of the victims of racist attacks, targeting not just individual racists but also the organisations they belong to. In 1987 the United Klans of America was bankrupted by a civil case the SPLC brought on behalf of the mother of Michael McDonald, a black man lynched by Klan members. More recently the focus has shifted to include legal challenges to anti-immigrant legislation.

Penny told me that, as well as its legal work, the SPLC has been involved in anti-racist campaigning. It produces a regular bulletin, "Intelligence Report' which identifies and 'outs' hate groups in the USA. The SPLC has identified over 1,000 such groups and as a result is universally loathed by right-wingers across the country. The organisation has also established numerous educational programmes promoting racial tolerance for use in schools.

Security was heavy and visible around the Memorial and the SPLC buildings and Penny had seemed quite suspicious on first meeting me, initially offering just a brief 10-minute interview. The security is understandable given that the SPLC building was fire-bombed in 1983 and the organisation's staff get frequent death threats.

Originally from the Mississippi delta, Penny has worked with the SPLC on and off since the 1970s. I ask how she thinks things have changed in the South over that time and whether she's optimistic for the future. Her answer is guarded, citing as a measure of progress the fact that the current chief of the state troopers in Alabama is black, but adds that in her social life she tends to stick with her own circle of friends, giving the impression that progressives here are an embattled minority still.

In that context it's admirable that the SPLC exists. I look at the impressive and costly building the organisation operates from in downtown Montgomery, and the commercial approach to the work that it implies, and scratch my head. But when you read about the cases the SPLC is pursuing (at the moment it's representing 'guest' forestry workers cheated out of their wages and mounting legal challenges to the use of pepper spray to control schoolchildren) and you can't help but be glad they're in business.

Downtown Montgomery is a riddle I never solved. I found large civic buildings, car parks reserved for this or that public organisation, but nothing that resembled an actual city centre - cafes, shops and the like – though the signs say, and Henrietta confirms, that I'm 'downtown'. Maybe I was just unlucky. Incongruously though, there was a handful of pretty rundown traditional clapboard houses cheek by jowl with the grand state capitol building, which I imagine the city hall bigwigs must hate. I speculated on whether the SPLC had brought a court case to stop the state from pulling these houses down.

My other main reason for being in town is to visit the Rosa Parks Museum. Rosa Parks was the woman who sparked the civil rights movement in 1955 by refusing to give up her seat on a Montgomery bus to a white man, so sparking a long and successful boycott campaign.

As I arrived at the museum a group from the Louisiana Leadership Institute, a black self-improvement youth organisation, was about to take the guided tour and I was encouraged by the museum staff to tag along with them and pay at the end of the tour.

The museum is exemplary. The focal point is an actual 1950s Montgomery bus onto the windows of which is projected a reconstruction of the bus ride that Rosa Parks took in 1955. From a technical point of view it works a treat, as testified by the rapt attention paid by the youngsters next to me. At the moment that Rosa Parks refuses to give up her seat as instructed by the bus driver (who was well-known as a virulent racist to the black community in Montgomery) there's a mixture of suppressed gasps and cheers from them.

I learnt from the museum that Rosa Parks was not the first black person to have been arrested for refusing to give up their seat in Montgomery; this had happened several times before. Segregation on the buses was particularly hated because of the demeaning way it operated. Any black person had to give up their seat to any white if told to do so. An elderly black person could be asked to give up their seat to a white child or youngster and would have to sit at the back of the bus. A black person had to pay their fare to the bus driver at the front and then enter the bus by the back door. Some of the more enthusiastic racists amongst the bus drivers got a kick from to driving off as a black person got off the bus to walk to the rear. This had happened to Rosa Parks before. A bus ride was a daily, public slap in the face for blacks in Montgomery.

The response to Rosa's arrest was remarkably well organised, as was the bus boycott itself. She was arrested on a Thursday evening, and by Friday evening over 50,000 mimeographed leaflets calling for a boycott of the buses had been run off and circulated around shops, workplaces and homes.

The boycott lasted a year with an elaborate alternative transport system, consisting of a fleet of station wagons, established to help people get around. When the operators of the station wagons were harassed off the streets by the local police, people walked wherever they needed to go; long distances in all weathers. The bus company put fares up for white passengers to compensate for the loss of revenue, so whites stopped using the buses too, which were now running empty. The black community had city officials and the bus company by the throat. In December 1956 a court ruling declared segregation on the buses unconstitutional.

It seems to me that this was a fight just waiting to happen. The church where Martin Luther King preached from 1954 to 1960, and the parsonage he lived in (which was bombed during the boycott) are a stone's throw from the Alabama state capitol building and close to the spot where Rosa Parks made her stand. Rosa herself had been politically aligned for some time and was an office holder within the National Association for the Advancement of Coloured People. Successful political activity is rarely completely spontaneous, even if it can seem so on the surface. The civil rights leaders and 'foot soldiers' (I was to find out later that this was what activists in the movement called themselves) chose their ground well.

I have to end this post as I started, with an apology, this time to any music historians reading this. The Hank Williams Museum and Memorial is in Montgomery. Hank was a native of the city and much as I wanted to pay my respects – without Hank Williams there would have been no Elvis Presley and no rock and roll music – I was all museum-ed out at this point and time was pressing. I tried to make it up to the old boy by playing him on the iPod as I left for Selma.

SELMA

While I'd been in Montgomery, driving round one late afternoon/early evening I'd heard a loud siren, very similar to the knocking-off hooter I used to hear as a child living in Hillsborough. It was called a hooter in Sheffield but it sounded like a siren. The knocking-off hooter came from the steelworks lower down the Don valley (clustered around what's now the ring road out to Barnsley) and could be heard all the way up the side of the valley and marked the afternoon shift change. It was a sound I'd heard only rarely since my childhood.

Driving in torrential rain a little while later a flash of lightning which went from one side of the horizon to the other, lighting up the town for a moment, gave me a clue as to the nature of the siren. You've probably got there before me – it had been a storm warning telling me that my best bet might be to get somewhere safe, preferably in a cellar, hunker down and wait for the storm to pass.

This was the first outbreak of the many storms that had passed through the south during that April and had caused such devastation. Montgomery must have caught the back end of one of them. I think this first outbreak had caused most devastation in Virginia on the east coast, although later storms were to break out across Mississippi and Alabama after I'd been through there, taking an even greater toll of life. The problem seems to be that the storm warnings often go unheeded because spring is storm season and warnings aren't that unusual. There'd been plenty of people out on the road at the same time as me in Montgomery who presumably weren't under the impression that the siren was a knocking-off hooter but continued about their normal business anyway.

Even the severest of storms can develop very quickly, touch down and rip through just a few neighbourhoods before dying out. In the previous outbreak something like 150 separate tornados had touched down. Most passed through lightly populated areas – much of Alabama and Mississippi is unpopulated or lightly populated – but some had hit neighborhoods and if this happens at night, or if the configuration of the land in a particular area is such that the tornado is only spotted at the last minute, there is little chance of escape.

Selma is just a short hop from Montgomery, 50-60 miles or so. I'd wanted to come to Selma to see the Edmund Pettus Bridge. It's a nothing bridge really, carrying Highway 80 into this small town, but in 1965 images of peaceful civil rights protestors trying to march from Selma to Montgomery being beaten and tear-gassed by police here had made their way onto our family's television screen and had set in concrete in my mind and in the minds of many others the reality of a struggle that had until then been vague and distant.

I arrived in Selma on a Saturday afternoon and as I settled into my new motel room I realised that I ought to check out opening times at the National Voting Rights Museum, the main purpose of my visit here.

My planning had let me down. According to my guide book Saturday closing time at the Museum was 3.00pm and it was now 2.20pm. On the off-chance my book was wrong I rang the museum. The woman at the other end confirmed the closing time but she must have heard the disappointment in my voice, leading to the following conversation;

> WOMAN: "Where you from?"
>
> ME: "From Montgomery... Sorry, I mean England. I'm travelling across the States and I'm just in town today and tomorrow." (I thought this might play better.)
>
> WOMAN: "How far away are you?"
>
> ME: "About 10 or 15 minutes" (I had no idea how far away I was but banked on the fact that nothing in Selma could be more than 10 or 15 minutes away).
>
> WOMAN: "Come on over, we'll wait for you."

I was met by Annie Pearl Avery who, as well as offering to show me around the museum, floored me when she explained that in 1965 she'd been one of marchers on the Edmund Pettus Bridge when the police had attacked.

That day hadn't worked out well for Annie. It was unlikely that I'd have seen her on our black-and-white TV all those years ago as she was probably the first marcher to be arrested. She told me that she had had a "physical disagreement" with one of the cops before the march had reached the bridge and had been hauled off to jail. The more I talked with her, the more this story seemed to sum Annie up.

Annie told me that she'd become involved with the Students Non-Violent Coordinating Committee (SNCC) in 1961 when she was just 16 years-old. Electrified by the news that the 'Freedom Riders' (black and white civil rights activists who rode interstate buses together to challenge segregated facilities) were coming to the South, she was too impatient to wait for them to get to her hometown of Birmingham, Alabama. She was determined to leave Birmingham behind to meet the freedom riders in Atlanta, Georgia.

After she'd been chosen to go on her first ride Annie decided to buy a few personal effects for the journey, and a knife to defend herself. The coordinator of the Freedom Rides campaign, Wilson Brown, found out about it and told her that the non-violent philosophy of the movement didn't allow for weapons, even in self-defence. Annie didn't agree with this philosophy and rather than submit to it she went back to Birmingham. Two weeks later however, after talking to Wilson Brown further and because "it seemed as if things were moving along", she accepted that the knife had to go.

Four years of activism with SNCC followed during which Annie told me she had been thrown in jail more times than she could remember. She recounted one time in Danville, Virginia, when the judge hearing her case took a prolonged nap during proceedings. Annie and her co-defendant took exception to this, walked to the front of the court and threw themselves on to the floor in front of the judge's bench. She got the judge's attention alright, and 90 days in solitary; 'contempt of court' the judge called it. And she served every one of the 90 days because she could only be freed on the judge's say-so.

We talked about the leaders of the movement for a while. Annie told me that she had been happy to work alongside the religious leaders of the movement but had never considered herself religious, and still doesn't. I asked whether she went to church meetings. "Of course" she replied. Out of necessity everyone went to church because it was the only place blacks could hold meetings without having them physically broken up. One thing she's still sure about is that it was the youngsters in the movement who pushed things forward. Martin Luther King and what Annie referred to as the 'mature' elements in the leadership always wanted to move cautiously but the youngsters wouldn't wait and the leadership often had to run to catch up.

We bring the discussion up to date. Annie is anti-war; "things still need fixing here" she says. Her ambitions for today's youngsters are decent health care, education, jobs and for them to be "culturally endowed". With regret we have to break it up as the museum, of which I've seen nothing, is belatedly closing. We walk out to the wreck of a car that's waiting for her. I wonder how she manages to drive the car with all the junk that's in there.

Before I left Annie had a favour to ask of me. We'd discovered a common interest in history as we'd been talking and she wanted to know more about the Civil War and the Reconstruction period which followed. Without a hint of self-consciousness Annie asked if I could find a book for her on the subject. I took her contact details and promised to dig something out and post it on to her.

She reminds me strongly of some of the elderly leaders of the tenants' movement in Sheffield that I worked with in the 1970s and '80s. Most of them were women, old members of the Communist Party like Betty Holden and Jessie Taylor, who were active in the tenants' movement before it was neutered by the council. Just like Betty and Jessie back then, the brightness in Annie's eyes remains undimmed, her curiosity unsatisfied.

Annie was 68-years-old when I visited her. Standing 5'3" tall and walking with difficulty she still possessed an air of indomitability.

The next day I visited Cahawba. You could call Cahawba a ghost town except that there's little or nothing of the town left for a ghost to haunt. The site is eight or nine miles south of Selma, in what is now beautiful, open countryside, but for a few years in the 1820s Cahawba (or Cahaba) was the state capital of Alabama. It quickly became a commercial and transport centre for cotton being shipped via the Cahaba and Alabama rivers south to Mobile on the Gulf Coast.

Cahawba's fortunes sank when the state capital was moved to Tuscaloosa, but there was a further influx of people and wealth when the railroad was extended to the city in 1859 (grand plans were made to make the city the 'New York of the South'). The place finally sank without trace during the Civil War when the railroad and the county seat was transferred to Selma, which sat on a more advantageous position on the Alabama river.

Freed black slaves tried to make a go of it here both politically (using the partially-ruined old state house to hold political meetings) and economically during Reconstruction, but by the 1870s they too had abandoned the city.

In a way, Cahawba stands as a testament to the dynamism of US capitalism in the days when the frontier was expanding westward. The vast natural resources of the country were still plentiful and towns and cities were being sculpted out of the wilderness. The remarkable thing is that within a few years of its abandonment little or nothing was left of the city. Because of the many opportunities to make profits elsewhere its physical infrastructure – bricks, iron, machinery – was simply lifted up and taken away and recycled into other projects. By early this century the place had practically been erased from the map.

Cahawba stands in stark contrast to what I had seen on my train ride from New York. Land and capital standing idle and abandoned because the opportunities to make a profit out of it are dwindling. However rich it might still be, the ailing capitalism of America in 21st century America stands in stark contrast to the youthful vigour of America in the 1800s.

It's still possible to make out the original lay-out of the city streets here, but structurally only the columns which once supported the Crocheron mansion (belonging to a successful merchant of the city who moved on when the money ran out) and the old slave quarters, are still standing. And the old 'negro burial ground' is still in existence; blacks and whites were buried in separate sites in the old South.

When I arrived at Cahawba, the park ranger was around doing a few odd jobs even though it was a Sunday morning and he should have been enjoying his morning off. Possibly he was nervous about his job; historical sites like this are under constant threat from swingeing state and federal budget cuts. We got to talking and like a number of other people I'd met he took a stab at guessing my nationality from my accent. 'Scottish' was his confident prediction despite the fact that I was sailing as close as I can to the Queen's English without sounding like a 1950s Home Service presenter. This set us off on an unfortunate conversational route.

The park ranger says he meets a lot of Scots who are unhappy at being called English. I tried in a couple of sentences to untangle the constitutional knot that holds together the countries that form the British Isles. As my clarification quickly floundered I resorted to a short cut by explaining that the powers devolved to Wales,

Scotland and Northern Ireland are the rough equivalent to states' rights in the US. Big mistake. Encouraged by my throwaway comment, the ranger launched into a disquisition on the Civil War (or the 'War for Southern Freedom' as he preferred to call it) and, smiling conspiratorially, thanked me on behalf of the whole of the sunny South for England's support in the war. Smiling back but sensing a row in the offing I told him that

> a) I wasn't around at the time
>
> b) England was deeply divided over the war.
>
> c) Many working people in the north of England collected money in solidarity with the Union cause and opposed slavery even though it may have been against the immediate economic interests of many of them.

An extended silence descended, both of us still straining to smile. You could hear the tumbleweed rolling down what used to be Cahawba's main street. Given that there was only me visiting this place (again) and that there were probably just the two of us within a 10-mile radius it was an extremely awkward moment. A little fancifully it flitted across my mind that he could dump both me and the hire car in the deep, muddy Cahaba river and nobody would be any the wiser, but the moment passed. The ranger remained the essence of southern courtesy and broke the silence by wishing me a great day. I wished him the same right back.

Relieved, I set off for Memphis. Via Sheffield, as strange as it may sound.

ALL THE WAY TO MEMPHIS

TO MEMPHIS

- PART ONE

ALL THE WAY
TO MEMPHIS

PART ONE

Until I reached Selma I'd been heading directly west, but my plans would now take me in a swing to the right up through the beautiful wooded hills of northern Alabama, to Memphis in south west Tennessee, back down the Mississippi delta following the river south for a way and finally back east to pick up the Natchez Trace Parkway and eventually down through Jackson, Mississippi, northern Louisiana and into New Orleans. The route was a kind of elongated figure 9.

I'd always planned on going to Memphis and I could easily have taken the I-98 interstate from Birmingham north-west to Memphis via Tupelo. I could give a number of passable reasons for what was, in effect, a sizeable detour to go due north on the I-65 and then cut across west but I didn't, and all because of my love of maps.

I've always loved looking at maps. The political, not the physical kind, maps with cities and borders on. You must have played that game where you step from one side of a border to the other, 'Now I'm in Yorkshire, now I'm in Derbyshire', or maybe you've gone to the end of a road for no better reason than to see what's there. I love all that. So, studying a map of the USA one day as a schoolboy I hunted for, and to my surprise I found, a place called Sheffield. It's in northern Alabama. I was really taken by this at the time and wondered what the place looked like compared to the Sheffield I knew. I vaguely promised myself that if I ever got the chance I'd go and find out. This trip was my chance to keep a promise.

Sheffield, Alabama, is one of three small towns on the south bank of the Tennessee river – the other two being Tuscumbia and Muscle Shoals – whose urban sprawls have connected up to form the 'Shoals' area. My passable excuses for being here were to visit the Helen Keller museum and the Alabama Music Hall of Fame, both in Tuscumbia.

The broad outline of Helen Keller's story will be known to many. She was born at the end of the 19th century into a prosperous, well-connected Confederate family. Her mother was related to US President John Quincy Adams and Alexander Graham Bell was acquainted with the family. Her father was at various times the proprietor and editor of the local newspaper, The North Alabamian, a solicitor and a US Marshal for North Alabama.

At a tender age Helen was taken by an illness which left her deaf, blind and totally without speech, although her physical ability to speak wasn't impaired. Her struggle to learn how to communicate, with the help of Anne Sullivan a tutor hired by her parents, who became a lifelong friend, has been the subject of a number of books and, in the 1960s, even a film. On her death in 1968 Helen was buried in Washington National Cathedral alongside such notables as Woodrow Wilson.

I'm telling you all this to explain the reason for my museum visit, because I recalled reading in an article a number of years ago that Helen Keller was for much of her life a militant socialist, pacifist and feminist. She opposed the First World War, joined the American Socialist Party and the militant Industrial Workers of the World (Wobblies) union. I was curious to see how this part of her life is portrayed. It came as a disappointment, but probably no surprise, that none of this was reflected in the museum. Not a jot. Absolutely loads about Helen's religious beliefs and charitable works later in life but this important part of her life had been air-brushed out of history.

After our group had completed the museum tour I questioned the guide about the omission. You've heard the expression 'farting in church', well I'm afraid that's what the guide's expression told me I'd done. Farted in church, belched in the vicar's face and spat on the collection plate to be precise. Once she'd recovered her composure, the guide explained that Helen's lively intellectual curiosity had led her to investigate a broad range of ideas and this was just one of them. The clear implication being that her flirtation with left-wing ideas was no more than a youthful indiscretion.

I've done a bit of research since which tells me that this isn't exactly true either. In 1955, at the age of 75 and at the height of the McCarthy witch-hunts, Helen caused a stink by sending birthday greetings to Elizabeth Gurley Flynn, an old comrade from the IWW then serving a two-year prison sentence for conspiring to overthrow the US government. Some flirtation.

As well as dancing around borders, you may well have wished moments in your life back again to deal with them differently. When I dug up this information I wanted to go back and confront the guide in Tuscumbia with a sneer of triumph. Unfortunately for me I was 700 miles away when my detective work came to fruition. That guide was damned lucky.

Arriving in my home city's alter-ego, I hung around the 'Welcome To Sheffield' sign on the edge of town pretending to do stuff but really waiting for a pedestrian to come by so I could ask them to take my photograph standing next to the sign. Some chance. Waiting for a pedestrian near a US highway is like waiting for an ice cream van in the Sahara. Passing drivers were staring at me because I was hanging around the 'Welcome To Sheffield' sign for no discernible reason. It was all getting a bit uncomfortable.

After a couple of purposeful-looking but totally unnecessary hikes back to the car to get things I didn't need I spotted a lone pedestrian, initially no bigger than a dot on the horizon. And he was walking in my direction. I was praying he didn't take a turning before he reached me but trying to avoid studying his movements too intently either. It was a very tricky business. When he eventually arrived I pounced on the young lad who'd become my saviour. He was happy to oblige me with a couple of photographs.

As he was on foot and seemingly heading in the same direction as me, I offered a lift in return for directions to the city centre. I'd been short on conversations for a while and a companion would make for a pleasant interlude, however brief. My lift's name was Jerome. He told me that he was a native of Tuscumbia but had settled in Ontario, Canada, a few years ago. He'd returned for an extended visit to introduce his kids to his birthplace.

> While we were talking it dawned on me that I'd driven at least a couple of miles and we were still short of his, and my, destination. I asked about public transport, Jerome smiled and told me it's non-existent. As his car had been left behind in Canada, Jerome had had to walk everywhere while he'd been on his visit. But it seems unthinkable there could be no public transport as we'd been driving through the heavily populated suburban area between Tuscumbia and Sheffield. I asked how older people and people with disabilities manage but Jerome just shrugged. He's an Ontarian now.

Later in the day I drove into the centre of Sheffield which, like a number of other places I've been to, seems down on its luck. There's an archetypal small-town American water tower before you reach Main Street, where shop front after shop front is empty. The Ritz, a fine old building, reminds me for all the world of the faded film theatre in 'The Last Picture Show'. I stared at it for the longest time taking photograph after photograph and half expecting Ben Johnson to exit the place, locking the doors behind him.

This isn't the image the city fathers are trying to project. In their website imaginings the area is a semi-rural idyll but Sheffield, Alabama, named after my home town, also shares its industrial history. The town was founded and grew after the discovery of local iron and limestone, its first mayor was one of the owners of the Sheffield Land, Iron & Coal Co and the Sheffield Furnace Company was a major employer here at the turn of the 20th century, running five blast furnaces. The town thrived during two world wars and in between it suffered through the Great Depression along with the rest of America. It wouldn't be fair to draw too many conclusions on the basis of an afternoon visit which took in little more than Sheffield's fading Main Street, but it's sobering to think that 20,000 workers had been drawn here during the economic boom which accompanied the First World War while today only 9,000 people live here, just a quarter of them working in manufacturing and construction. This is the precarious economic base on which the town operates.

> It had taken the best part of 50 years but I'd made it to the dot on the map I'd stared at as a youngster. My impression as I left was that Sheffield, Alabama, has many of the same problems as its namesake.

The Alabama Music Hall Of Fame tells the story of the two recording studios which together brought the 'Muscle Shoals' sound to the world. The FAME (Florence Alabama Music Enterprises) studios and publishing company were founded by musician and producer Rick Hall in the late 1950s. He hired local session musicians who developed the soul and gospel-inspired studio sound which attracted Paul Simon, Bob Dylan and countless others to record here.

Four members of the original rhythm section that Hall recruited – Barry Beckett, David Hood, Jimmy Johnson and Roger Hawkins – went on to found the Muscle Shoals recording studios in Sheffield. Both FAME and Muscle Shoals studios are still active. It's guaranteed that anyone with the slightest interest in music will have bought a single or album recorded here at one time or another and I would have loved the opportunity of a look round one or both of the studios but time (I'd allowed myself less than a day here) worked against me. I should at least have taken a photograph before leaving though. Chalk up one more planning failure.

Alabama has more than its share of musical heroes who are recognised at the Music Hall Of Fame and I decided to write them down. It's a long list including Hank Williams of course, Emmylou Harris, Nat 'King' Cole, Wilson Pickett, Erskine Hawkins, Eddie Floyd, Sam Philips, Toni Tenille.

Whoa, hold up. Toni Tenille? Yep, Toni Tenille. One half of the Captain & Tenille who had just one UK hit to my knowledge with the inoffensively catchy 'Love Will Keep Us Together' in 1975. The Captain & Tenille are bigger in the US than in the UK it seems.

This really puts a crimp in my visit and I wonder whether the Hall Of Fame has a Court of Appeal. I can put together a strong case for ejection;

- *Count one; their name is just ridiculous.*

- *Count two; 'The Captain' has this thing where he wears a nautical hat. Only Count Basie is hip enough to wear a nautical hat and get away with it.*

- *Count three, and this is the clincher; their website enthuses about Toni's 'dynamic vocal stylings'. Do me a favour: re-listen to 'Love Will Keep Us Together' and read that phrase again.*

I get the strongest feeling that it's time to move on.

ALL THE WAY TO MEMPHIS

PART TWO

Memphis grabs you in the same way as New York does. It's not just the music scene, as good as that is. It feels like a proper city with different points of attraction for people with different interests, different means and different lifestyles. In Memphis you can point to the posh bit, the bohemian bit, the suburbs, the bit where people aren't doing so well. In a number of the cities I'd visited the knot of roads surrounding them seems to have strangled their individuality and killed downtown.

I had arrived in Memphis at night which was unfortunate as I'd hoped to avoid driving in a big, unknown city in the dark. Henrietta was on the money though, and got me there without sending me the wrong way up an expressway ramp – a recurring nightmare.

One of the first things I asked my new host, Jenny, was about using public transport to get around Memphis but she dismissed it immediately. The transport company is practically broke she told me, as is the city, and the buses are completely unreliable so I'd have to use the car for my visit to the Sun and Stax studios.

The next day I wondered, open-mouthed, into the Sun recording studio. This is the holy grail. Rhythm and blues, country and gospel walked in the front door of this building and rock and roll burst the back door off the hinges, screaming and howling on its way out. The flow of popular music came right through this building where I'm standing. The place is perfect. It even smells like you'd expect a studio to smell, which to me means it smells like my auntie's old reel-to-reel tape recorder. It may smell this way because it's still a functioning studio at nights.

We were told by our enthusiastic, entertaining and informative guide Eldorado (or it could be El Dorado; either way he's got terrific sideburns if you're into that sort of thing) that the performance area is exactly as it was for the historic recording sessions of the 1950s, as is the office, which has a battered old Remington typewriter sitting on the desk as proof. There are crosses on the floor where Elvis, Bill Black and Scotty Moore are said to have stood when they made musical history. Only the actual recording booth upstairs has been updated.

It's a fairly well known story, but Eldorado confirms it. Sam Philips, head of Sun Studios, wasn't overkeen on Elvis's voice to start off with. Sam was a blues man and always said that the best voice he ever recorded, including Elvis, was Howlin' Wolf. Elvis sang a sappy ballad for his demo and Sam pulled up some way short of impressed. His secretary persuaded him to let the kid hang around the studio because she thought he'd got something. Looking at photographs of Elvis from the mid-50s it's not hard to guess what she thought he'd got. It was only when Elvis, Bill and Scotty broke into an impromptu upbeat version of a country ballad called 'Blue Moon Of Kentucky' that the fur started to fly.

I took lots of photos of the backs of people's heads while we were all milling around in the studio. Eventually we were shepherded outside and I persuaded someone to take a photo of me with an inane but contented grin before I dragged myself away.

And then on to the Stax studio museum. In the 1960s Stax was the vital gritty counterweight to Tamla Motown. If Tamla was the clean-cut boyfriend you took home to meet mum and dad, Stax was the bad boy who took you out in his car on the sly. So while Tamla's Jimmy Ruffin was wondering "What Becomes Of The Broken Hearted?", Stax's Johnnie Taylor was posing a more down-to-earth but possibly more urgent question, "Who's Making Love To Your Old Lady (While You're Out Making Love)?".

From the early 1960s to the early 1970s one soul masterpiece after another by the likes of Otis Redding, Wilson Pickett, Booker T & The MGs, Sam & Dave and Eddie Floyd was recorded at the Stax studios. Stax had a distribution deal with Atlantic records until 1968, so most of the classic singles and albums on the Atlantic label before that date would have been recorded here. A shaky deal with Atlantic, followed by another with CBS, contributed to the label's decline. The company filed for bankruptcy in 1975.

The original Stax studios were demolished in 1989 and the place was re-built in part to try and breathe life into this rundown part of Memphis. If my initial impressions were anything to go by it's only been partly successful. If Bedford-Stuyvesant was working class black America, the area around 'Soulsville USA' looked like minimum-wage or no-wage America. I parked up on an empty lot in front of a boarded-up shop. As I was leaving an old guy with a limp and a walking stick called to me: "Wouldn't leave it there if I was you. That guy's lowdown." After a bit of clarification it turned out that the owner of the land I was parked on just loves ticketing unwary drivers who park here even though the land's no longer in use. The old guy told me that 15-20 cars were ticketed at a festival held at the Stax museum the previous weekend.

I thanked him for the information, we fell into conversation and he asked me where I was from. When I told him I was from the north of England he disclosed that he was in my part of the world as a youngster, playing rugby. I have to admit I was sceptical but when he told me that he played as a winger and as a running back in American football, ("weighed 220lbs, ran 40 yards in 4.4 seconds") and that his job as a winger was to make as much ground as he could and set up a ruck, I started to believe him. I suggested that it must have been rugby union he played. He confirmed that it had been rugby union and told me how he'd once played against a Welsh team. Then he shook his head as if reliving a bad memory, "They were nasty, boy, nasty". By now I was convinced.

THE CRADLE OF ROCK 'N' ROLL

I was surprised to find that the museum is one part of a complex that also includes a charter school and a college of music, part of the same redevelopment plan that included the renovation of the studios. This bit of the area is a hive of activity with lots of students from the college and school making their way around a small campus attached to the museum. A surface impression again, but it struck me as impressive that this oasis of learning has been put together, with its facilities open to local children, in such a run-down area.

The museum itself is really well presented. There is wall after wall containing original singles and albums produced at Stax. Record collectors of a certain age could spend an entire afternoon playing the "Wow, I used to have that single, I wonder where it went" game.

The Stax studios (with the original sloping floor, the building was a cinema before it was converted to a studio) have been faithfully recreated but the centrepiece for me was the restored, peacock-blue 1972 Superfly Cadillac El Dorado complete with television, refrigerator, and gold trim, once owned by Isaac Hayes. The car is on a rotating plynth so you can see every last shiny piece of chrome in glorious detail.

Back in the sixties and seventies this car must have been a real head-turner. It's conspicuous consumption for sure but it's also a statement of black pride, Isaac Hayes' way of saying, "I'm black and I've made it."

The tour starts with an award-winning 20 minute documentary in which many of the leading artists at Stax talk about what those days meant to them. The Stax team, including Jim Stewart and Estelle Axton who owned the studios, were unselfconciously multi-racial. White and black played, wrote and produced together. "It wasn't an issue" is a sentiment that's expressed on film a number of times. But they also agree that the murder of Martin Luther King and the riots that followed put an end to the closeness of their working relationships ("It was never the same again") and contributed to Stax's decline.

As an aside, and to show what a gloriously creative jumble the music of the South has always been, both Steve Cropper, white guitarist with Booker T & The MGs (which was effectively the Stax house studio band) and veteran black soul singer Rufus (Walking The Dog) Thomas cite the long-running country and western radio show 'The Grand Ole Opry' as a major influence when they were growing up. Rufus Thomas gets all excited just talking about tuning in to listen to it.

It was late afternoon when I emerged from the museum, brand new Stax T-shirt in hand, and I decided to drive downtown before night fell. By following the noise I found Beale Street. I strolled round absorbing the music coming out of the many bars on this famous 200-yard long strip, joining the many fellow tourists and members of the Memphis constabulary who were here to keep a friendly eye on us and to make sure our money went into the joints it was supposed to go into.

The Rum Boogie Cafe called to me (B.B. King's club looked a bit plush and I was feeling dishevelled from touring all day). In short order I was sat at the bar nursing a beer, eating red beans and rice and listening to J.P. Soars & The Red Hots. Actually the band was OK but definitely not red hot. A three piece blues-rock band, they were more rock than blues to be honest. J.P. played lead guitar and tended to go on a bit with the solos, making them a bit one-dimensional. But, there are times when context is everything and this was one of them.

After listening to a couple more bands from the street I wandered off in search of the lobby of the Peabody Hotel which in legend marks the northern end of the Mississippi delta. It turns out it's just a hotel lobby. Eleven o'clock in the morning is the time to be here I found out later. Tradition dictates that every day a flock of geese are paraded round the lobby at that time. No, I don't know why either, but it's a nice tradition.

There was a bit of a gale that night. One or two really strong gusts shook the house and made the lights flicker. Jenny's dog Queso had made a friend of me and came into my room when Jenny wasn't home, which was most of the time. Queso slunk under the table with his ears flat to his head when the going got rough and I wanted to join him. I could feel a power to this storm that I'd never felt at home and the violence of it set my heart racing on a couple of occasions.

In the morning I walked to the car to find that a couple of trees had been felled, one of them blocked off one end of the road, another had written off a house porch. Thankfully nobody seemed to have been injured. Queso had had the right idea after all, though I'd had to draw a firm line in the early hours when he'd tried to get in bed with me.

I'd set myself a hard pace in the early part of the trip and was starting to feel it, but I couldn't visit Memphis without visiting the National Civil Rights Museum. The NCRM is based in the Lorraine Motel, the site of Martin Luther King's assassination in 1968. The motel, and even the rooms where King and his entourage stayed, have been kept in pretty much the same condition as at the time of the assassination.

The museum presents an exhaustive, and exhausting, account of the civil rights struggle going back to the 18th century. The museum tells how black people were treated as property under US law until 1787; in that year the US Constitution declared that each black man was equal to three-fifths of a white man for the purposes of taxation and representation in government. I made copious notes of bits of information like this, much to the curiosity of my fellow visitors, but the main thing I took away from the museum is that the threads of continuity within the civil rights struggle may have become stretched at times but they never broke.

In 1891 black citizens in Louisiana challenged the state ruling that whites and blacks had to travel in separate railway carriages when Homer A. Plessey, foreshadowing Rosa Parks, was arrested for riding in a white carriage. The Supreme Court backed the state of Louisiana. It took almost 100 years to put that right.

There's more evidence here of the bravery of individuals in the face of state power. In 1932 Angelo Herndon, a 19-year-old southern black Communist (triply cursed), joined a march of out-of-work Georgia labourers demanding the resumption of suspended relief payments. He was arrested, tried and convicted of inciting insurrection and sentenced to 20 years imprisonment. After a long legal battle Herndon was released in 1937 and immediately took up his political work again. People like this are hidden from history.

I was so taken with Herndon's brief appearance in the museum that I stood in the semi-dark, acutely conscious that I was being stared at by everyone who came past, and wrote down a long quote of his;

> "I don't know if I can get across to you the feeling that came over me whenever I went to a meeting of the Communist Party... All my life I'd been sweated and stepped on and Jim Crow-ed. I lay on my belly in the mines for a few dollars a week and saw my pay stolen and slashed, and my buddies killed. I lived in the worst section of town and rode behind the 'colored' signs on streetcars as though there was something disgusting about me. I heard myself called 'nigger' and 'darky' and had to say 'yes sir' to every white man whether he had my respect or not.
>
> I had never known that anything could be done about it.....and here I had found organisations in which negroes and whites sat together and worked together, and knew no difference of race or color. Here were organisations that weren't scared to come out for equality for the negro people and for the rights of workers... It was like all of a sudden turning a corner on a dirty old street and finding yourself facing a bright shining highway."

On my last morning in Memphis I went out with my camera. I have a fascination with deserted buildings and I'd learnt that in Memphis city centre there were a couple of monsters that had been deserted for decades. It was too good an opportunity to miss.

The Sterick building is an abandoned 30-storey skyscraper slap bang in the middle of downtown. At 350,000 square feet it would dwarf most buildings but it's been empty since the 1980s. I almost picked up a ticket from a very friendly (once he realised I was a tourist) traffic cop while I was photographing it.

I can't improve on my guide book's description of the Sears Crosstown building: "Blotting out the midtown sun like something from a Tim Burton film, this 1.4 million square feet department store headquarters is too expensive to redevelop or tear down. Built in 1927, it's been abandoned since 1993." I visited it on an overcast, rainy day, which was the perfect setting. It's colossal and eerie. I counted 89 windows from one end of the building to the other. I wondered what it must be like to wander round such a place, and whether Tim Burton had discovered it.

MEMPHIS TO NEW ORLEANS

Actually I did one last thing before I left Memphis. For a while I'd been debating with myself whether or not to go to Graceland. My instinct was to give it a miss, on the grounds that if Sun studios symbolised the young, vital Elvis, Graceland symbolised the bloated, karate-suited, jaded Elvis. But a couple of people had said they had done the tour and I should give it a try. My compromise position was to have a wander round outside, take a couple of photographs and see how things went.

Things didn't start well. A $10 charge to stick my car in the official Graceland car park did nothing in the way of softening my prejudices and despite the exorbitant charge Graceland was nowhere to be seen from the car park. I spent a little time wandering round something called the Heartbreak Hotel (which is officially on Lonely Street according to the city's street sign) wondering if it was Graceland, decided it wasn't, transferred my attention to this other large building a little way distant which turned out to be the entrance lobby/ticket office/memorabilia stand for the real thing.

Graceland itself is a gated compound which the designers of Guantanamo Bay would have a wet dream about. Taking a photograph of it without paying for a tour ($30 for the basic go-round) would have required a gymnastic ability and disregard for personal safety which isn't built in to my genes. Neither did I want to tour Elvis's car collection or his personal planes (you pay separately for these tours). So I passed on all of them, had my photograph taken with one of Elvis's cadillacs which stands outside the entrance lobby – just to prove I'd been there – and took my leave feeling slightly more ill-disposed towards Elvis the elder than I'd been on arrival.

From Memphis, Highway 61 takes in the Mississippi Delta and the heart of blues country. My first stop was to be Clarksdale, just 60 miles or so down the road. (Own-up time – before I researched this trip I'd always assumed that the Mississippi Delta was at the mouth of the river where it meets the Gulf of Mexico. In fact, Delta country is that part of the Mississippi river flood plain on the eastern side of the river about 350 miles to the north of where I'd assumed it was.)

I set out for Clarksdale. Highway 61 runs parallel to the river and just a few miles to the east of it, so the influence of the Mississippi is strong and the countryside is dead flat. Cotton fields either side of the highway initially look like mud flats at this time of year (in contrast to the red clay soil of Northern Alabama, the earth in Mississippi is deep brown, almost black) until you get sideways on to the direction in which the field has been ploughed and can see row after perfectly parallel row. I tried to gauge the size of the fields under cultivation by trying to estimate the number of football pitches you could fit in each but it's impossible. 200, 300, 500? Your guess is as good as mine.

The fields have been planted and prepared but the cotton isn't in bloom at this time of year. In a few weeks' time I suspect all around here will be white from horizon to horizon.

As my journey is a short one I decide to turn right off the main highway for a while. I'm rewarded for my initiative by a sign that tells me that by turning left I can follow 'Old Highway 61' which looks as if it runs south parallel to the highway I'd been on. The old highway takes me through poor townships and isolated shotgun shacks with rusted cars littering front yards. (Shotgun shacks are so-called because they have a door in the front and another door directly facing the front door in the back, so a shotgun could be fired through the house without hitting anything).

As I drove I speculated that the huge planted cotton fields all around here would deliver a sizeable income for someone, but not for these people living next to them. I was so busy taking in this rapid change in scenery that I didn't notice that I'd lost Highway 61 to my left, the one I'd been driving on originally. I found this a little alarming but I was quietly confident that there'd be a sign directing me back on to the highway. A few miles further on a bridge appeared - a large bridge. It was a large bridge because it spanned the mighty Mississippi. This was particularly alarming as my route should have run parallel to the river, not over it. There was no turning back now though. Over the bridge and past a sign which read 'Welcome To Arkansas'! Arkansas was in no way part of the plan. An outside observer would have noticed a slight slump in my shoulders right about now.

Truth to tell though, having spent a full 40 minutes or so in Arkansas, I can report that it's a very friendly state. Within a couple of miles there was a Welcome Centre with rest rooms, tour information, a complimentary coffee on offer and a chance to regroup. A quick check of the map reassured me I wasn't wildly off track (albeit that I was in a state I'd never planned on visiting), the day was still young and the coffee was good.

A smiling member of staff gave me the inside track on what Arkansas has to offer and pressed a collection of guide books thicker than a Gideon bible into my hands. I didn't have the heart to tell him I was heading back to Mississippi the instant I stepped into my car. I decide to keep the guide books for any friends considering visiting Arkansas. I thought it was the least I could do for the state that had put a comforting arm around me when I was at a low ebb.

I drove guiltily but determinedly back into Mississippi, promising myself that there'd be no more detours today.

The place I stayed in Clarksdale was called the 'Shack Up Inn' and was rumoured to be a little different. It was so different that I drove past it twice before I realised it was my lodgings. The place is an old, rundown, rusted cotton gin that's been converted internally but left in its abandoned state externally. There are rusting pieces of farm machinery, old cars and the remains of grain silos all over the grounds. I was in Bin No. 5.

That night I headed downtown to explore the 'Ground Zero Blues Club'. Sitting at the bar in the 'Lady On The Levee' restaurant prior to the music I was the recipient of a hearty slap on the back which almost resulted in my catfish going down the wrong way. It was Madge. Madge was under the impression that I was someone that I'm not, to wit a friend she was dining with that night. Madge apologised for her mistake but decided to engage me in conversation anyway as her husband and their dining partners, one of whom looks like me from behind apparently, hadn't shown yet.

> *Like so many Americans I'd met Madge was engagingly enthusiastic. She was particularly enthused to talk to me about business opportunities in Clarksdale and the Delta but sadly I couldn't rise to the challenge of reflecting her excitement. Undaunted, Madge pointed out a group of men in the restaurant who had come all the way from Sweden to their little town. Then turning to another group in the restaurant she whispered, in excited yet reverential tones, that they were from California. Again I failed to step up to the plate, simply nodding and smiling. Valiantly, Madge passed over her business card and asked what business I was in. Something died a little in her eyes when I told her I'd been in public service all my life and the conversation finally fell off the edge of the cliff that it had been teetering on for so long. To the relief of both of us her company arrived shortly afterwards.*

Every spare inch of the walls of the Ground Zero Blues Club was covered in graffiti. Some big names have appeared here, but tonight local performers were on stage – The Evil Love Band. The band are young and workmanlike and are just putting together their first CD. The bass player plays in a long poncho-like coat and bare feet. It seems like they've brought their own following as they circulate round most of the people in the bar between sets.

Their first set was followed by a jam session. A guest singer going under the attention-grabbing nickname 'Razorblade' took the stage to lead the band in a couple of soul-inflected numbers. Bearing in mind his nickname, he got a hearty round of applause from me. Actually he was pretty good and I could have listened to some more numbers from him.

Next to be welcomed to the stage was a group all the way from...Sweden. It was the group from the restaurant. The irony wasn't lost – I'd come thousands of miles to the heartland of the blues to listen to a band who'd travelled even further than I had. The lead singer's spoken English carried a heavy North European inflection when he introduced the band, but he offered up an almost perfect Delta delivery as soon as he started to sing – a tribute to the power of the blues. And they were actually pretty good, stacking up well against the local blues bands I'd heard so far. I never caught their name though.

Passing the time of day with the 'Shack Up Inn' receptionist as I checked out the next day I complimented her on their place and told her that I would have stopped another night if I hadn't been on such a tight schedule. "Well you can't anyway" she snapped, taking me a little aback. "The whole place is being taken over for a wedding. They're from California". She busied herself with my paperwork and as she did so repeated, absent-mindedly and seemingly to herself , "They're from California". I began to form the impression that Californians, or at least the ones who can afford to drive out to Mississippi for a wedding, form some sort of aristocracy round here."

On my way out of town I spent a little time at the celebrated crossroads where Robert Johnson is reputed to have sold his soul to the devil in return for his remarkable ability to play the blues. Quite apart from doubts which naturally arise from an account of the devil assuming bodily form to play fast and loose with a musician, questions have been raised as to whether these are the actual crossroads that Robert Johnson was referring to. Apparently the precise site of Mr Johnson's encounter with Lucifer vary with every telling of the story.

No Matter. The crossroads mark the intersection of Highway 61 and Highway 49, two roads closely associated with the blues tradition and it's right in the centre of Clarksdale. These crossroads will do as well as any.

I'd reached the bottom part of my figure '9' loop now, travelling south east to Indianola, Mississippi, birthplace of B.B. King, and then on to Canton, also in Mississippi. I stayed overnight in Indianola, an attractive little town with a bayou running alongside main street. I didn't have much luck in Indianola. I decided to go for a walk by the bayou only to find that within 10 yards I was in someone's garden, and trespassing is very much frowned on in these parts.

I had hoped to catch a band in town. Unfortunately, lack of persistence on my part meant that I missed out. That night I wandered round the downtown area for quite a while but couldn't find either of the clubs my research had dug up. A quick tour by car the next morning on my way out of town turned up both of the clubs (the Ebony Club, bought up by B.B. King when it was in danger of going out of business, and Club 308). When I got out of the car to take a photograph of the Ebony Club frontage the family living next door to the club, who were out on the front porch swing taking the Saturday morning air, enquired after my health. We exchanged pleasantries and I asked if there had been a band playing the previous evening and I was told that indeed there had been. The young lad in the family warned me that I didn't ought to be messing in there after 11.00pm at night though. "The old folks go in about 6.00 or 7.00 and leave at 9.00," he advised, for future reference.

Somewhere between Indianola and Canton the Mississippi river loses its grip and I started to climb through low-lying hills. Canton is way off the tourist track. I was there because it's within striking distance of the Natchez Trace Parkway. The Parkway is a scenic two lane road that roughly follows an old trading route running from Nashville in the north to Natchez in the south. It's a bit like driving through a National Park if you can imagine a National Park running from Aberdeen to Dover – Natchez Trace Parkway is over 440 miles long.

The history of the region is signposted at regular stops along the route. The story is a familiar one of how the Choctaws who had settled the land around the old Natchez Trace were bullied and swindled out of their land.

There are plenty of activities to engage around the Parkway – nature trails, camping ("Stinkin' Jim's Campsite" is publicised heavily but doesn't recommend itself from the name), horse riding and biking. If this bit sounds like a travelogue it's because I know a few families who would lap up the Natchez Trace Parkway. It's run by the good folks of the U.S. National Parks Service who also host a very informative website.

I was planning to cover the bottom quarter of the Parkway on my way to meet my wife, Carol, in New Orleans and set out from Canton for a reconnoitre the day before. It's a strange, anachronistic but rather wonderful experience driving the Parkway; the speed limit is a strict 50mph (at the top end it's 40mph) there is NO overtaking and you share the road with joggers, cyclists and a fair sprinkling of superannuated Hell's Angels giving their Harley Davidson's an airing. Trees crowd up to the edge of the road, branches practically brushing the roof of the car in places.

I stopped off at River Bend, overlooking the Pearl River. It was a Sunday afternoon so people had just started to set up picnics and barbecues. There were speedboats cruising up and down the river, a couple of the speedboats had water-skiers attached. Later I found a place, Cypress Swamp, that I'd spotted on the map on one of the dark evenings when I'd been planning the trip. It's a short nature trail just off the Parkway and it seemed strange to be here after seeing it on the map on our kitchen table so many months before. I'd got here at the right time, just as the heat was going out of the day. I was alone, and apart from frogs bellowing and crickets clicking it was one of those rare times in life when there's absolute, complete, utter silence.

Travelling further to the Ross Barnett Reservoir I met Shannon. He was fishing off a jetty on the reservoir and we struck up a conversation. Shannon had a heavy southern accent (he pronounced 'wind' as 'weeyund') and I was having trouble keeping my accent under control too, so it was a little heavy going at times for both of us.

I discovered that Shannon doesn't work – he's on a disability benefit because of a chronic respiratory complaint. He told me that he used to be a painter, of the decorating rather than the artistic kind. When I asked whether his disability could be related to his occupation he just said 'maybe' and fell silent. I didn't ask whether he was in the union when he was working because I was fairly sure what the answer would have been.

Shannon hunts as well as fishes. His hunting licence costs $16 a year for which, providing he abides by the appropriate rules and regulations, he can hunt on public land anywhere in Mississippi. His love of hunting seems as natural to him as breathing in and out. He hunts deer, squirrels, possums and rabbits. He eats what he catches and particularly loves the taste of deer. The more we talk the more I can see why hunting would seem like the most natural thing in the world to him. When I tell him that only the rich go hunting in Britain he finds it very hard to believe.

Shannon told me that he has only ever been out of the county he was born in (Madison County, Mississippi) on a couple of occasions. He asked me how I'd got there, did I drive or fly?, and in the context of the conversation it seemed to me that he was asking whether I'd flown or driven to America from Britain. It may have been a simple misunderstanding, but my reticence prevented me from pursuing the question any further.

Speaking of accents, the cleaner at the Canton motel I stayed in said to me one morning, and it was a statement rather than a question, "Y'all from Russia ain't ya." I think a few of the staff at the motel had been having a discussion and had reached a consensus about my provenance. I added Russia to the growing list of countries that I'd been associated with while I'd been over here.

TALES FROM THE FOREST

1. I did the hundred-and-odd miles down the Natchez Trace Parkway the following day doing between 40 and 50mph with the iPod on shuffle and with the road to myself nearly all the way. Bliss.

2. I saw a big black snake basking on the path in front of my car as I pulled off the road. I was so excited I dropped the camera on the car floor as I was getting it out of my pocket. The snake slithered away into the undergrowth unphotographed so I'm afraid you'll have to take my word for it.

3. A coyote crossed the road in front of me. Cocky bugger it was too. Stopped and turned to look at the car before sauntering off – like one of those students who take no notice of your approaching vehicle and stroll across the road daring you to clip the back of their legs with your bumper. I tipped my baseball cap to the coyote; cocky students usually get a less generous greeting.

NEW ORLEANS

There was a tearful reunion with Carol at New Orleans airport (we'd never been apart for such a length of time) and a tearful parting 10 days later, but the time in between was joyful. A number of Carol's friends had told her that to get the most out of our stay we would need to learn to just *be* in New Orleans, and that turned out to be very good advice.

Everything about New Orleans is unlikely and exceptional. Eighteenth century French colonists had the bright idea that an unpromising plot of land at the mouth of the Mississippi infested by alligators, snakes and mosquitos, an area prone to hurricanes, floods and malaria, would make a splendid hub for trade up and down the river. The city was founded on slave labour, its earliest residents were Canadian backwoodsmen, engineers, prostitutes, troopers, drifters, craftsmen and convicts. Its fortune was built on King Cotton. Growing wealth attracted French creoles, free people of colour and emigrés from across the Caribbean. In the 19th century political control of New Orleans bounced between France and Spain until the United States government bought the place for peanuts.

Not surprising then that New Orleans can seemingly be anything you want it to be. It is effortlessly elegant in parts, the French Quarter and the Garden District are as graceful as you would wish any big city to be. It can also be tawdry. Though there's still good music to be found there, Bourbon Street with its packs of frat-boys, convention-goers on the loose and shop-front skin joints, seems to have sold its soul.

In adjoining shops you can buy pieces of fine art or a junk T-shirt announcing "OBL-DOA" (Bin Laden was finally tracked down by the US armed forces while we were in New Orleans). You can try and re-live the city's halcyon days by travelling down the mighty Mississippi on the steamboat Natchez (the last paddle steamer on the river) or take a sobering look at the havoc wrought here by the elements with the connivance of George Bush's administration. Hurricane Katrina laid the Mississippi Gulf Coast to waste, but only caught New Orleans a glancing blow. The flood was a man-made disaster as the locals will tell anyone who cares to listen.

In New Orleans you don't have to go and find the music, very often it just comes to you. As we were strolling down a sidestreet one day a group of seven or so youngsters came towards us, playing as they walked. They were a street band; by their direction of travel I guessed that they were on their way to play in Jackson Square but seemingly they couldn't wait to get there to get started – the music was just bursting out of them – so they were playing and walking and smiling.

Not all the street music that you hear is jazz, with or without the syncopated 'second line' New Orleans rhythm that the city is famous for. At various times we stopped to listen to classical music, blues (of course), folk and country.

My favourite street musicians did play in the New Orleans style though. 'The New Orleans Street Band' played in Jackson Square and had tourists, winos, interested locals and possibly the Square's pickpockets joining in the fun. They twisted the Temptations' "Just My Imagination" and The Beatles' "Come Together" gloriously to their own ends and out of all recognition from the originals. I'll never be able to listen to those songs again without thinking of Jackson Square.

We went to see Big Al Carson at The Funky Pirate on Bourbon Street. Big Al sings his own brand of lewd, lascivious blues backed by an excellent, stone-faced band. Al is a showman and makes up for the backing band's passivity by doing things with his lips, mouth and eyes that, frankly, a man of his age would only get away with in a blues club. He leaves little room for misinterpreting his lyrics. There's no cover charge to go in but the bucket is passed round on 3 or 4 occasions during the night so the band does OK. Our evening on Bourbon Street was rounded out very agreeably by Dwayne Burns and band who played and sang in the Louis Armstrong style at the Maison Bourbon.

Looking through the local paper one night I chanced across the information that The Iguanas were playing in town. I'd bought a second hand copy of one of their albums years ago just on the strength of their name and the look of the album cover (one of the lost joys of shopping for music in the age of downloading) and loved their blend of rock, rhythm and blues and traditional Mexican music. I'd forgotten they were a New Orleans band but when we saw they were playing we put on our glad rags and went down to The Chickie Wah Wah to catch the show. They were mesmeric, just about the best bar band I've seen. Carol went so far as to say they played the best show she's ever seen, full stop, and went up and told them so right after the gig. The stand-out performers are Rod Hodges, who plays lead guitar and accordion and shares vocals with Joe Cabral, whose saxophone solos brought the house down. At the end of the night I realised that this was one of the reasons for making the trip. Bands like The Iguanas have just too localised a following to be asked to play in Britain. Our night at Chickie Wah Wah's made me an evangelist for this band. If you get a chance to listen to their music you should.

Another band worth evangelising about is The Meters. They're one of the quintessential New Orleans outfits. Starting up in the '60s, they can justifiably lay claim, along with James Brown, to have pioneered funk music. For contractual reasons I imagine, they're now called The Funky Meters and we were dead lucky to catch them performing at Tipitina's.

The band has a stellar New Orleans line-up of Art Neville on keyboards, George Porter Jr on bass, Brian Stoltz lead guitar and Russell Batiste on drums. They didn't seem to have a set list as such, but with curt nods and sideways glances the music flowed from one number to another without a discernible gap between, building a tension in the room that became almost unbearable. What they do is the musical definition of 'infectious' and I found, dear reader, that I had to dust off my creaking hips and grab a piece of the dance action.

Art Neville had been grumpy all night long though. He'd started a version of "What'd I Say" and then abandoned it a little way in because he didn't think the crowd were responding vigorously enough. George Porter Jr had spent the night playing alongside him to jolly him along, but Art abandoned the first song of their encore, said he'd had enough and was off.

Carol had also abandoned me, temporarily but understandably, when the hip-shaking started. I eventually caught up with her in a scrum of revellers outside Tipitina's. It was a recommendation from one of the group to visit Frenchmen Street that led us, a couple of nights later, to this hub of music just two blocks long which I found infinitely preferable to Bourbon Street. In the space of about 150 yards we watched three bands, any one of whom would have been worth spending a full evening with:

> • *Sunpie Barnes And The Louisiana Sunspots at Mojito's – delicious cajun, blues and reggae. You couldn't spot the join...*
>
> • *The New Orleans Jazz Vipers – trad jazz with vocalist. More lively than you'd imagine. It got the crowd at The Spotted Cat jumping around anyway.*
>
> • *Wolf & Roosevelt – young guns playing hard-edged blues with a dizzying assortment of guest players to help them out at The Cafe Negril.*

> *As an aside, my observation is that playing and listening to music isn't the same in the States. Audiences are transient; many will come to the bar, have a beer, maybe two and move on. This is even more pronounced in cities like New Orleans and Austin where bars jostle endlessly for the music lover's dollar. As a musician you could be playing to a completely different crowd at 9.30pm than the one you were playing for at 8.30pm. People are still drifting in to listen to music at 10.30/11.00pm on a weekday. We sat and watched Wolf & Roosevelt for a good long time and my guess is that they warmed up three completely different crowds in the time that we were watching. It must be a hard school for a musician to learn in.*

Finally, we went to the Jazz & Heritage Festival, one of the highlights of the musical year in New Orleans. In truth I think it's fair to say that neither of us enjoyed listening to the music at the festival as much as in the bars, which may have something to do with the lack of intimacy at an outdoor event.

There was nothing wrong with the performers mind you:

- *Keb' Mo' – clean-cut, precise blues and straight pop.*
- *Henry Gray And The Cats – Chicago blues. Henry may now well be the oldest of his generation of blues piano players still around after the death of Pinetop Perkins, erstwhile pianist in the renowned Muddy Waters band.*
- *Mount Zion Pilgrim Baptist Church Choir – gospel. They might just get me into church if they came to sing in our neighbourhood.*
- *Warren Storm with Willie T. & Cypress – old school Cajun with some rock 'n' roll thrown in.*
- *Tab Benoit – Louisiana blues.*

And last but not least, for a few numbers at the end of his set, gnarled old Robert Plant. He was headlining but I don't think his folky offerings were really connecting with this audience. Melancholic cries from the stage of "Come down to the front" and "Is there anybody out there?" suggested that the artist wasn't happy. Actually he was getting a reasonable reception but not an ecstatic one, which is what a superstar rock performer comes to expect.

When I thought of all those talented jobbing musicians in the New Orleans bars playing for tips after a day at work, competing with the TV and the band playing across the street it was hard to have too much sympathy.

We took in a minor league baseball game which was a real All-American family occasion. Hot dogs, fizzy drinks and the traditional rendition of "Take me out to the ball game" during the seventh inning stretch. The New Orleans Zephyrs played the Oklahoma City Redhawks. We were supporting the Zephyrs of course and thanks to our support they ran out 10-7 winners, including a Zephyrs' grand slam (the ball was hit out of the park with the bases loaded so 4 runs were scored from one hit) from left-fielder Josh Kroeger. And we got in free because the family in front of us had spare tickets.

To finish, a quick word about New Orleanians based on a very small sample. We only had chance to listen to two local voices for any length of time; both were tour guides and both were fascinating, fast-talking (which must help if you want to be a tour guide), opinionated, knowledgeable and altogether admirable in their own way.

Joel took us on a swamp tour. He's been in the army, been a fisherman and hunted most things that move in Louisiana – particularly alligators – for a living. We learned that he hates (not necessarily in this order); the government (he calls them the feds), health and safety (he drinks water straight out of the garden hose on the grounds that the minerals in it help to fight his cholesterol), climate change theorists and political correctness. He speaks with a knowledge and passion about preserving the Louisiana wetlands and coastal areas that's hard to deny. And the need for preservation is a very practical one; the wetlands area acts as a 'speed bump' for hurricanes like Katrina blowing in from the Gulf Of Mexico and it seems that they and the coastal areas are disappearing at an alarming rate.

> *Joel tells amusing stories that may or may not be true. Like the time that a snake fell from a tree branch hanging over his tour boat into the middle of a group of pensioners who all forgot their arthritis and did a jig before jumping onto the boat's benches. Or like the time he got bit by an alligator he was luring up to the boat. As he was struggling to get the beast to release its grip tourists were gathering round with their cameras asking him to face them so they could get a better shot. Or like the time he was asked whether he has pet names for the orphaned baby alligators he raises. His response; "Hell no. I didn't even wanna name my kids."*

Kathy, who took us on the Katrina tour had, shall we say, a more balanced approach to the ills of New Orleans; she berated the developers who had moved in and made a killing from buying up cheap land and property that the victims of the flood couldn't afford to move back to. She shared Joel's distaste for a government which had refused to give grants to people who couldn't provide the title deeds to their house after Katrina had made them homeless. Louisiana state law makes it expensive to transfer title deeds, even within families, and many families in the mainly black areas that were worst affected by the floods didn't have deeds to their house even though the house had been bought and paid for generations ago.

Kathy also shared Joel's sense of being exceptional in hailing from New Orleans. Seemingly, New Orleanians see themselves as different to the rest of the USA, indeed to the rest of Louisiana. Joel kept referring to himself as a south Louisianan. Kathy explained a number of times how people in New Orleans are different. The unique history and racial mix of the city must lend support to the idea.

There's an understandable sense of fatalism about New Orleanians. Joel has been evacuated more times than he cares to remember. Last time he almost didn't return. He did come back, but that doesn't mean that he and Kathy don't think something bad is going to happen again to New Orleans.

After 10 days in this flawed pearl of a city I returned to Louis Armstrong airport with Carol, but she was flying east to go back home and I was flying west, to Corpus Christi, Texas.

TEXAS GULF COAST

The sign on the plane to Corpus Christi said "Continental Express" with the "Express" in italics just to prove how fast we were going to go. I wasn't convinced judging by the plane, which groaned, rattled and wheezed its way over Texas. The young American sitting in front of me was returning from a tour of duty in Afghanistan and this was the fourth and final leg of his journey back. As we flew closer to Corpus Christi he started to twist and turn in his seat looking out of the window for familiar landmarks after being sent to the other side of the world.

As it was only a couple of dollars more per day than an 'economy' I'd reserved what was billed as an 'intermediate' car with the hire company but the vehicle that was waiting for me in the airport car park resembled a Sherman tank. It was, by European standards, a huge SUV. I couldn't see the steering wheel from outside the car without craning my neck and I had to reach up to put the door key in the lock. Everything's bigger in Texas.

I'd chosen to fly west from New Orleans to Corpus Christi for a couple of nights as it was by the ocean and would give me a chance to take stock and plan the rest of my journey. I'd picked my motel because it was right by the ocean but I'd not done my homework properly. There was a monster of a dual carriageway – North Shoreline Boulevard – between me and the shoreline. Think of Scarborough with the A1 for a promenade. I was happy to move on after a couple of days.

I didn't know this until I started researching the trip, but America has barrier islands all along its Atlantic and Gulf coasts. My next stop was to be Port Aransas (known as 'Port A' to the locals). It's a town of some 3,000 people (although that can swell to many times that size at the height of the tourist season) at the tip of Mustang Island, one of the most southerly of the barrier islands along the Texas Gulf coast. Mustang Island in turn is connected to Padre Island, said to be the largest barrier island in the world. Between them, the two connected islands have a beachfront on the gulf side stretching some 165 miles.

No doubt there are plenty of second home-owners and people in the tourist trade here, but Port A's permanent population seems to consist mainly of fishermen, retirees, hold-out hippies and people who've had bellyful of it on the mainland and want a slice of life in the slow lane. My kind of town in fact.

My host was Carol Elliott. Carol worked as a musician in Nashville – where she made five albums – and Fisherman's Wharf in San Francisco. She told me she'd appeared at the Cambridge Folk Festival. One of the nights I was there Carol sang for a mainly local crowd on the porch of The Tarpon Ice House, a local bar. The sun was just starting to lose its heat; it was the perfect setting for the 1970s confessional singer-songwriter material that's her speciality. It's a fact that people either love or hate this stuff. I'm happy with it when it steers clear of self-indulgence which, happily, Carol's set did.

Carol's boyfriend is Ronnie Narmour. He'd worked for many years in the music industry in Austin 'buying and selling talent' as he puts it. Booking and promoting bands might be a less brutal job description. Ronnie had been on first name terms with a lot of the musicians I've only ever gazed at on album covers – Doug Sahm, B.B. King and others – so I was intrigued to hear how he ended up here.

> One of Ronnie's chief claims to fame is that he's played poker with bluesman Albert King. It seems the cards weren't running for Albert on the night they played, so much so that at one point he had to ante-up his pipe to stay in the game. Ronnie was also keen to let me know that Kim Wilson of the Fabulous Thunderbirds (lead singer of the most consistent R&B band of the last 30 years) still owes him $120 on a deal. He was a little shy of giving me the details of the deal.

Booking and promoting bands is a hard business to be in and the time came when Ronnie decided enough was enough. A friend of his runs the local newspaper here and a quick phone call put him in the car and on his way to a new life as the music correspondent for the local paper, 'The Island Moon'. Port A has a lively music scene for a small town and Ronnie had settled at the heart of it.

To my eye this is a handsome place. The houses come in all sizes and a host of pastel colours. Some, like Carol's, have unpainted wooden exteriors. Swiss-style chalets compete for attention with bungalows, trailers and frame houses. Some houses resemble a ship's bridge in construction. Others, in fear of flood, are built on stilts. Some of these houses have a 10 feet void below them, which becomes a completely open basement storage area. Climate change raises the possibility that Port A may disappear in the not-too-distant future.

Walking round the port and the town is a treat for the senses. It's not a sleepy fishing village by any means but everywhere in town is just about walkable from everywhere else, which is a real novelty. If you want a speed rush you can hire an electric golf kart to get you about. Many of the locals have bought their own karts. The highest point on the island is six feet above sea level so many people cycle round town.

> I was watching the basketball play-offs in my temporary local bar one night when I got talking to Steve, a chef in the Castaways Seafood and Grill over the road. Steve evidenced a strong commitment to the institution of marriage in that he'd done it five times. I'd never met anyone who'd been married five times before and I was slightly in awe of him. Steve's story revolved round his first marriage to Lynn who hailed from Chelmsford in Essex. As the story began I shifted nervously in my seat a little thinking this may not go so well.

Steve and Lynn married and set up a fishing tackle business in California which was doing fine until Steve returned from a business trip one afternoon to find the shop closed up early, which was unusual. When he went home he found the house stripped of everything except his clothes. A quick dash back to the shop revealed that it too had been completely stripped. Further enquiries by Steve revealed that Lynn was back in Essex and had sold all their household possessions and half a million dollars worth of stock from the shop. I think most people would have one of two responses to this kind of crushing blow, either curling up into a tight ball or travelling to Chelmsford heavily armed. To his credit, Steve's response was to jump right back up on the horse – four times. "All four were Texas girls", he tells me. Unfortunately there were four more dismounts.

So Steve ended up in Port A with nothing except a camper van and a dog. Until his camper van caught fire. Passers-by who saw the dog running backwards and forwards across the top of the dashboard as the flames licked round his paws broke the windscreen and rescued the pooch. At this stage Steve would have been sleeping under the pier if a friend hadn't advanced him a month's rent for a trailer which, happily, he was still in.

Steve was a really gentle man. He showed no animosity towards Lynn or towards life in general. In fact at that very moment he had spotted a gap in the market for selling fishing tackle in Port A and he was working on a plan. I warmed to his benign resilience, so much so that as soon as we'd shaken hands and said our goodbyes I went straight across the road to the Castaways Seafood and Grill for my tea. I wanted to play a part, however small, in making sure that Steve had a pay packet at the end of the week.

There are no trees outside Port A to break the constant, cooling on-shore breezes which sweep across the island. The wide beaches are backed by large dunes. Marine grass dominates outside the coastal area. Like a much bigger and much warmer version of Spurn Point on the Humber estuary.

I need to tell you a couple of things about the beaches. Number one, you can drive on them, all of them. In Texas all beaches are public highways and all traffic laws apply. You drive on the right and there are speed warning signs (15 mph) all down the beach. If you get stuck in the sand it's your responsibility to get a tow out. I lifted the following advice to drivers directly from the website of the National Parks Service who administer the Padre Island National Seashore; "Watch for small children near the surf, where they cannot hear approaching vehicles." Number two, although nudity is illegal on Texas beaches, a federal law passed in February 2010 sanctioned the carrying of guns here. Where you would carry your gun, if you're wearing budgie smugglers, is a question that still haunts me.

I have to admit that early one morning, overcoming environmental reservations, I went for a drive on the beach. I pulled into a break in the dunes which fronted on to a cafe (no parking meters), had my scrambled eggs and coffee overlooking the ocean and drove back up the beach. I left my gun at home.

The next evening I was invited to go with Ronnie and Carol to see Davin (pronounced Day-vin) James at 'The Back Porch'. Ronnie was reviewing Davin and the band for the 'Island Moon' and thought I'd enjoy them. The Back Porch is an open-air bar right on the water. It was a mixed crowd on the night we went; married couples, out-of-towners like me, a birthday party and a group out on a hen night.

Davin James and his band are from Houston. They're a three-piece and play solid, hard-edged Texas country music. They can change things up though. I made a mental note of the first four numbers of their second set; New Orleans funk, a straight blues, western swing and a cryin' country song. Impressive versatility. I was sure Ronnie would give them a good write-up.

The biggest disappointment of my stay was that I never saw any of the local dolphins. I'd been told that they're regularly seen swimming and leaping in front of boats sailing the strait which divides Port A from the mainland, but an afternoon on Roberts Point Park, which overlooks the strait, produced no results.

There was some interesting, not to say slightly threatening, wildlife though; a group of six to eight large pelicans which flew slowly and menacingly up and down the beach on most days looking altogether pre-historic. Like a bunch of re-animated pterodactyls. I assume they were looking for food but I never once saw them swoop on anything, they just flew in convoy up and down the beach. I sunbathed with one eye open.

On my last afternoon it occurred to me that I'd not been in the ocean. There'd been warnings about jellyfish which had lodged in the back of my mind and could have played a part in keeping me on dry land but I couldn't leave America's 'Third Coast' without swimming in the Gulf of Mexico. It was more of a splash-about really as there were big breakers coming in. And when seaweed unexpectedly wrapped itself round my leg it became an undignified, frantic hop-about until I realised I wasn't being assaulted by marine life.

On my final evening here Ronnie used the internet to map out my music options during my stay in Austin, my next stop, and Carol helped to sort me out some accommodation there. (My forward planning had crashed in the absence of a wi-fi connection here.) This was the clincher. I'd really enjoyed their company anyway but this had to be my cue to break out the Henderson's. Tears were held back but I'm sure I saw lower lips trembling.

On the same day that I was heading north for Austin, Ronnie was in a car travelling the 170 miles or so south west into Mexico to have work done on his teeth. It would cost him peanuts compared to having the work done in the States. It seems like everybody who lives within striking distance of Mexico and has a passport does this.

I'm told dental surgeries line the streets in Mexican border towns. Many of these dentists are Americans who cross the border every day to practice. While I'm driving to Austin I conjure up visions of right-wing republican types down here complaining about the porous border while flashing their Mexican smiles.

AUSTIN

The road leading away from Port Aransas and towards south central Texas ran through a series of shallow, dusty, wooded valleys and even dustier south Texas towns with beautiful names like Tuleta, Seguin and Geronimo, over the Guadalupe River bridge into San Marcos, before eventually reaching the outskirts of Austin.

Passing through Kenedy, about 120 miles south of Austin, the car was registering 95°F outside and I was hungry and thirsty. I pulled over to the Taqueria Vallarta roadside cafe to experience my first 'Jalisco style' Mexican breakfast. The cafe's mid-morning clientele consisted of car mechanics, sales reps and office workers. The Taqueria Vallarta's memorable breakfast was justifiably ample for people who'd done a hard morning's work or, like myself and the reps, a long early-morning drive. Two pork chops, both almost as big the plate they came on, two fried eggs, potatoes, re-fried beans all spiced up with tabasco sauce. And as many coffee refills as you could handle.

There's an all-too-rare feeling of perfect contentment you get when a meal hits exactly the right note at the right time in the right place. I took the trouble to record my breakfast at the Taqueria Vallarta so that I can call up that feeling when memories of my trip start to fade.

Austin stands on the Colorado River and the road leading me in from the south ran through a green corridor leading almost as far as downtown, a welcoming introduction to the city which has the reputation of being a little out of step with much of the rest of Texas, adopting a more bohemian approach to life than is usual in the Lone Star state. 'Keep Austin Weird' is proudly emblazoned on lots of T-shirts here. I'd arranged to meet up with a group of socialists in Austin during my stay. The fact that there were people in Texas who called themselves socialists in itself said something about the city.

My lodgings were close to Zilker Park, which stretches from downtown into the southern suburbs. The park contains Lady Bird Lake (created by damming the Colorado River, named after President Lyndon Johnson's wife) and Barton Hot Springs which are said to maintain a steady 70° water temperature all year round.

My short experience of American cities suggested that opportunities for an urban lakeside walk might not come around too often, so I was happy to take the opportunity. Lots of other people had the same idea that day, a colossal number of calories were being shed in Zilker Park, involving countless ways of shedding them. There were dog walkers, casual walkers, power walkers, casual joggers, joggers with dogs, joggers with 3-wheeler baby chariots, cyclists with dogs as well as your serious, low body mass index joggers and cyclists. Of the seemingly thousands of Austin citizens out exercising the only one I couldn't categorise was the cyclist wearing nothing but a leather posing pouch. He had a terrific tan.

It's serious stuff this. So many Austinians are out and about getting fit in and around Zilker Park that a local business has had the genius idea of setting up watering stations around the place to improve its brand recognition. Joggers run on the spot passing the time of day with each other while they take water on board next to a big sign displaying the company name.

An outdoor fitness class was in full swing, as was a game of frisbee football. I'd heard about frisbee football but never seen a game and stopped to watch to work out the rules. Michael Parkinson once famously said that he'd watch two flies crawling up a window pane if it was a good race, a sentiment I can identify with.

The informal game I watched was played on a pitch marked out by cones to about the same length as a football pitch but quite a bit wider. There were nine players per side. The attacking player receiving the frisbee has to catch it cleanly to retain possession but can't run with it in his or her possession. Defenders only have to bring the frisbee to the ground to break up the attack and win possession. No offside rule and no goals. You score by catching the frisbee cleanly in the opponents' end zone, as in American football.

I'm no expert but the players showed a good deal of skill. They could throw the frisbee surprisingly long distances, make it hover for an eternity to give their team-mate the best chance of catching it, or deliberately curve it round a defender by throwing it at an angle. You have to be fit to play too, intelligent running to give your team-mate a chance to make a decent pass is as important in this game as it is in football.

I stayed to watch the game and hung around much longer than I intended to. The park and the lake were too beautiful to abandon easily on a sultry Texas afternoon. The waters of Lady Bird Lake have a soft emerald look from vegetation covering the lake bed. Turtles inhabit the lake and, when they temporarily lose their sense of direction, flirt with disaster on the paths around the lake. The bow waves of kayaks, stand-up paddle boats (surf boards with an oar) and rowing boats criss-cross the lake's surface. An idyllic time.

A wealth of excellent music has come out of Austin and looking through the weekly listings the range of live dates on offer was impressive. Ronnie Narmour had made a few recommendations while I was in Port Aransas, which I hoped to follow up. Mike Milligan was one of them. He was appearing at Maggie Mae's on 6th Street, which is Austin's equivalent of Beale Street and Bourbon Street. He's a tall, slim, good looking blues singer with a fine tenor voice, an extremely snappy dresser and dextrous blues harmonica player, maybe a little over-elaborate at times. His back-up band were three burly Texans who looked as if they'd just walked in from a day working on the farm, but they could play.

The Austin skyline is attractive with a small number of elegant skyscrapers visible from just about everywhere in the city. I had an afternoon wandering round downtown Austin before joining a protest outside the Texas State Capitol building at the top of Congress Avenue later in the day.

Abortion rights are under attack all over America. In Texas, the state legislature had passed a nasty bill which forces doctors to conduct a sonogram (what we know as a scan) at least 24 hours before an abortion. The doctor then has to show the woman the results of the sonogram, describe what the sonogram shows and force her to listen to the fetal heartbeat before the abortion can be carried out. The bill was still awaiting the signature of Republican Governor Rick Perry to pass into law when I was in Austin, but he was fully expected to sign it through.

The protest was a small one – maybe 60 or 70 people at most – but the strength of support from passers-by was an eye-opener. There seemed to me to be a level of support for a woman's right to choose in this most conservative of states which took myself, and possibly the protest organisers, by surprise. Every wave and toot of a car horn was greeted with enthusiastic whoops and cheers by the protestors. One of the protestors I talked to summed up the defensive nature of their struggle when she asked, "Didn't my mother win this fight already?" I met up with members of the International Socialist Organisation at the protest and stayed with them for the evening after the protest had broken up.

Times are hard for people with progressive political ideas, and particularly hard for people with an open commitment to socialism. Being small in number, the emphasis has to be on organising around specific issues alongside individuals and organisations who may not share the ISO's socialist politics. But the left is on the defensive here and I was told that protests like the one we'd just been part of are often called at very short notice, leaving little chance to mobilise larger numbers of people. Campaigns tend to spring into life for short periods and disappear without leaving much behind in terms of solid networks of people.

Unions are weak at the moment. Texas is a 'Right To Work' state, which you can interpret as a 'Right To Work For Less' state. Many of the people I met were working in the public services and are hamstrung by the Right To Work legislation. One woman who works at the University of Texas in Austin told me that she has to negotiate her pay individually with her manager and hasn't had a pay rise for several years. She added that her best hope of negotiating a pay rise is to secure a job with another employer on a higher pay scale, show the job offer letter to her manager and hope that will result in a pay rise. Even that might not work.

Ten thousand people had marched in Austin in March to oppose massive federal budget cuts which could lead to $10 billion being cut from the education budget in Texas and possibly a third of teachers' jobs going, but the teacher I spoke to had no legal right to strike to fight these cuts. You have to keep reminding yourself that despite the stifling right-wing consensus that dominates in the United States, a consensus that the democrats have barely challenged let alone broken, 45 years ago America was the birthplace of the civil rights, anti-war, women's rights and gay rights movements of the '60s. In the few months before my visit the city of Madison in Wisconsin had been shaken by big popular, militant mobilisations against anti-union state legislation, a much-needed reminder of this country's proud labour history.

You can hear and feel a simmering discontent here over a whole range of issues, most of which relate back to America's declining economic power and how free market, 'trickle down' economics has impoverished and burdened ordinary Americans. Whether that discontent will be channelled down a progressive or reactionary path in the long run is still an open question.

In the 1970s Robert Christgau was my music critic of choice. He wrote for the 'Village Voice' newspaper but I knew him through his 'Consumer Guide To Rock Albums Of The '70s' which conveniently rated albums from A+ to E- for collectors on limited time and a limited budget. He could praise or damn an album or an artist with a couple of well-chosen words.

Christgau had given decent reviews to a couple of albums by a band whose country hick name – Alvin Crow & The Pleasant Valley Boys – positively demanded further enquiry. But as hard as I looked I could never track those albums down, and then he disappeared from view. So Alvin's name jumped off the pages of the 'Austin Chronicle' when I read it, and I decided to renew my search. I tracked him down at Ginny's Little Longhorn Saloon, "The Home Of Chicken Shit Bingo", as the sign said over the stage. A real downhome Texas bar about the size of a scout hut. I noticed a large collection of 8-track cartridges on a shelf behind the stage which neatly summed the place up.

Alvin cut a striking figure in stetson, wraparound shades, grey/blonde dreadlocks and James Coburn smile. Switching effortlessly from guitar to country fiddle, he and his band played a mix of straight-ahead country covers and western swing, a variation of country music born in America's South West and drawing its inspiration from the big jazz bands of the 1920s and '30s. You'd normally expect to hear it played by bands with a horn section but this was a little unrealistic in Ginny's Little Longhorn Saloon.

Nevertheless, Alvin got the locals dancing alright (there was next to no room so they had to take it in turns) and a fine time was had by all. I drove all the way home with a big smile on my face, search completed.

GOLDEN GATE BRIDGE, SF

WITH ELS, TUCSON

ALVIN CROW & BAND, AUSTIN

PLEASE DO NOT THROW
CIGARETTE BUTTS IN URINAL
IT MAKES THEM SOGGY AND
HARD TO LIGHT.

SOUND ADVICE

ALIOTO'S
SABELLA / LA TORRE
THE Crab Station AT Fisherman's Wharf
Fresh Crab · Seafood Cocktail · Clam Chowder · Fried Seafood
No. 3 Fisherman's Wharf
Sab
LaTorre's
ORIGINAL FISHERMAN'S W
TOW-AWAY NO STOPPING ANY TIME
NICK'S

EMBARCADERO, SF

BAYOU COUNTRY

GROUND ZERO BLUES CLUB, CLARKSDALE

THE NATIONAL VOTING RIGHTS MUSEUM & INSTITUTE

WITH ANNIE PEARL AVERY, SELMA

HAPPY AS LARRY AT SUN STUDIOS

WITH JOE IN SF

SCI-FI SCULPTURE, EMBARCADERO, SF

SF GIANTS IN ACTION, AT&T STADIUM

POWELL AND MARKET

20

BAY & TAYLOR

ICONIC SAN FRANCISCO

FALLEN GIANT, SEQUOIA NATIONAL PARK

STRANGE ROCK FORMATION, MOJAVE DESERT

MT. MARIACHI SERENADERS, SAN ANTONIO

GHOST GROCERY STORE, MOJAVE DESERT

AUSTIN TO TUCSON

San Antonio rivals Austin for the title of premier city of south east Texas. The two cities, about an hour's drive apart, are joined by the I-35. The interstate is one big commercial corridor. Stores, motels, petrol stations, offices, and a jungle of tall advertising signs jostling for air space, run alongside the I-35, separated from it by side roads running parallel and giving six, seemingly eight at times, lanes of traffic frantically running north and south.

I had to return my hire car at San Antonio airport and catch the 'Texas Eagle' across the length of Texas to Tucson Arizona. Train times had left me the choice of staying in San Antonio one night or three and I'd opted for one. It was a choice I immediately regretted once I'd walked around the city, which retains a strong sense of its Hispanic and Mexican history. Many buildings from the Spanish colonial era are still standing, more recent constructions have been designed to blend in. Buildings are variously rust-coloured, cream, dun or terracotta. When the sun began to set and the blue sky turned pink the city looked a picture. Even the rail station was a beauty.

The centrepiece of downtown San Antonio is the Riverwalk. The San Antonio river was dammed and diverted after a disastrous flood in the 1920s and a pedestrian walkway was constructed alongside the diverted river at a level below the roads that run through the centre of the city. The Riverwalk is no doubt a hymn to commercialism with shops, bars, hotels and restaurants lining the pedestrian walkway and barges running tourist trips around the waterway. But it's easy to be seduced by the Mediterranean feel of the place. Restaurant tables line the edge of the river, early evening promenaders decide where to eat or simply come out to show themselves off.

I ate at one of the Mexican restaurants lining the Riverwalk and surrendered to the prevailing atmosphere by paying a Mariachi band $10 to sing to me at my table. I chose 'Perfidia', a long-standing favourite, as my request. The trio performing the song duties were 'Mariachi Mexicanisimo' and I can't deny that I hadn't really thought through how awkward it would be for all concerned for a lone male to be sung a love song by three mustachioed Mexicans in front of a full restaurant and scores of passers-by.

My eyes and those of the singer did a little dance with each other. We kept catching each other's gaze and then letting go as quickly as we'd engaged, both of us staring off into the middle distance. Thankfully for all concerned the relationship didn't catch fire, although I've since learnt that the last line of 'Perfidia' translates as 'I desire more kisses'. I really should have offered a tip for putting them through it.

There was a Mariachi festival that night and San Antonio is the perfect place (outside Mexico) for it, but the train to Tucson left at 5.40 am and it was an 18-hour journey. An early night was essential.

The 'Texas Eagle' was gently snorting and fuming on the platform when I arrived at the station the next morning. It had started its long journey in Chicago on Thursday afternoon, travelling south through Illinois, Missouri, Arkansas and Texas arriving in San Antonio on Friday night, resting overnight ready for an early Saturday morning start and continuing on through the Texas desert, New Mexico, Arizona and California, reaching Los Angeles early Sunday morning.

The sun came up on Texas farmland early in our journey, the low angle of the sun's rays catching the tops of the trees. Within two or three hours cultivable land had turned to semi-wilderness and then we were in the northern tip of the Chihuahan desert. No trees now, but straw-coloured grass on the flatlands interspersed with straggly green brush (probably creosote, acacia and tarbrush I found out later). Bushes here don't like to crowd each other; they find their own space to take best advantage of the little rain that falls.

We ran through flat terrain with stretches of low-lying hills, escarpments, cliffs and gulleys breaking up the monotony. Anonymous mountain ranges loitered politely on the horizon without impeding our progress.

I fell into conversation with Alejandro who I'd shared a table with at breakfast, along with a couple from New Orleans. Alejandro had not been particularly interested in talking at breakfast, but we got seated next to each other in the observation deck and he opened up a bit. He told me he was travelling to the end of the line in Los Angeles. Of Mexican descent (his father had never taken out American citizenship out of loyalty to the old country), Alejandro had been in the military and then the Correctional Service and had taken retirement at age 51. The prison job, in a juvenile facility, had started to get to him badly. I asked him what he did now that he was retired. "Nothing at all" he offered with a smile but no further explanation. A man of few words.

I wondered whether his military background explained how he managed to look so well-pressed even though he'd been travelling on the train for many hours and had slept in San Antonio station overnight to avoid paying for a room. We watched the Texas countryside roll past from our elevated position and noted the number of hides and lures where hunters wait for their prey. Although this land seems good for very little, there's plenty of fencing around, suggesting it belongs to somebody. Sometimes the lures and the hides seem to be just a few yards apart. We agree hunting here must be like shooting fish in a barrel and speculate that these Texas hunters must have poor quality rifles or be very short-sighted.

Our observations led us to a discussion about gun ownership, which Alejandro supports even though, since he retired, he has no interest in owning or carrying a gun. He found it hard to envisage a situation where gun ownership is as strictly controlled as it is in Britain and clearly saw such control as an infringement of civil liberties. I didn't argue, in part because I know it's of little use given the country's traditions and Alejandro's background, and in part because I wasn't altogether sure I disagreed with him.

Eight hours into the journey, at Alpine, Texas, we took a break to stretch our legs. El Paso, on the west Texas border with New Mexico, was still four and a half hours away. I told you everything's bigger in Texas. By late afternoon we were running close to the Mexican border. It was just possible to make out the Rio Grande as a thin, dark ribbon in the distance. The mountains a few miles to the south were in Mexico.

As we neared Tucson the train made an unscheduled stop and after a few minutes two armed cops and a third person, who I took to be a railroad official, boarded and made their way to the back of the train. They returned a little while later with a youngster in his teens or early twenties who was clearly at a loss to understand why he was being rousted by the cops. After a delay of about ten minutes the train set off and the whisper came back from the front of the train, hard to believe but apparently true, that the cops had been called in because the youngster had been playing his iPod too loudly and hadn't responded to requests to turn it down. The rumour didn't stretch to saying whether he'd stayed on the train or been thrown off.

I'm an agitated traveller by train at the best of times and when our journey extended way past the scheduled arrival time in Tucson I unpacked my mental worry beads. There'd been a brief, unannounced stop about half-an-hour before, was that Tucson? Had I somehow missed my stop? Phoenix, the next major stop, was 118 miles further down the tracks. An announcement from the porter that we'd entered a different time zone, the clocks going back an hour when we crossed from New Mexico into Arizona, came just moments before meltdown.

Alejandro was on the station platform when I gratefully clambered off the train in Tucson. We shook hands and I promised to look out for him if my planned visit to his hometown of Ventura, just north of Los Angeles, came off. Alejandro smiled politely, neither shaken nor stirred.

TUCSON

TUCSON

Tucson lies on an elevated plain surrounded by the Sonoran desert and the Santa Catalina, Santa Rita, Tortolita and Rincon mountain ranges. I was corrected by a Tucson native for describing the space between the mountains occupied by the city as a 'plain' and told that I should call it a valley. I'm sure that must be technically correct but the term 'valley' doesn't conjure up the right image; this valley is pretty flat and possibly 40 or 50 miles wide.

Driving through the city from the airport, where I picked up my third and final hire car, there was an immediately different feel about Tucson. The air seemed clearer here, the view sharper. Tucson feels like a city in the sky, although we're only at an elevation of 2,300 feet. The city is expansive, even by US city standards, but then again there is more than enough elbow room here for the city to have a good stretch. Four-lane expressways run through the suburbs but happily not through the downtown area which retains an old-town charm. The city has only one building over 100 metres and 20 storeys in height, Austin has 14. This is the sort of thing I look up so that you don't have to.

The Sonoran desert is the home of the saguaro cactus – the tall ones with arms that you see in all the western movies – and this stately cactus is everywhere you look here, adding a distinctive, if not unique, look to the city. My lodgings were in an affluent suburb on the north east of Tucson, in the foothills of the Santa Catalina mountains.

I'd recently read a book called 'Jack Ruby's Kitchen Sink' by Tucson resident Tom Miller. The book tells stories of unusual occurrences in the south west border region. One of the chapters in the book recounts the sad story of David Grundman, who went out into the Sonora desert with a friend, both of them full of booze and bravado and intent on shooting up an undefended saguaro cactus. Saguaros are huge, reaching up to 60 feet in height and weighing over 2 tons when fully hydrated. Grundman apparently peppered one of these gentle giants with gunfire but was unable to topple it. Moving in for the coup de grace he picked up a stick from the desert floor and, jumping up, poked at one of the heavyweight arms of the wounded cactus in an attempt to detach it. Unfortunately for the befuddled sharpshooter, the heavyweight saguaro arm that he eventually prised loose chose his head for its final resting place, killing him outright. Tom's book has been re-issued under the appropriate title 'Revenge Of The Saguaro'.

I'd been so taken by this, and Tom's other stories, that I'd tracked down his email address and asked if I could meet up with him. To my surprise (and no little consternation) he'd agreed.

Before meeting Tom though I had a date with the Santa Catalina mountains, or at least a small portion of them. Els, my host in Tucson, had recommended Sabino Canyon in the eastern part of the Coronado Forest as a good starting point. Trolleys run visitors up the four-mile length of the high-sided, saguaro strewn Sabino Canyon. The trolley driver who drove us to the head of the canyon had one of the most eccentric deliveries I've ever heard, addressing us very slowly as if we were a pre-school group and stressing the end of each sentence just to make sure we'd taken it in. I imagine that if you had to cover the same four miles of territory telling the same story several times a day for a long enough period, any strategy for easing the boredom must help but it was noticeable that our driver had a perfectly conventional delivery when not doing his pre-planned talk.

At the head of the canyon I jumped off the trolley ready to walk back down. It was late afternoon, the sun was dipping behind the mountains and there was a sweet breeze blowing up the canyon. Nobody else was tempted to join me. As soon as the trolley left I realised how alone I was. The guide had said that mountain lions, bobcats, coyotes and javelinas (a small hog-like animal) inhabit the mountains, though the chances of meeting any of them are, he said, slim.

Almost as soon as I set off walking I heard something definitely approximating an animal noise, a noise which was magnified by the narrow canyon and I instinctively let out a curse. It was a deep grunting noise, suggesting a javelina, the least threatening of the creatures the guide had mentioned. For a while afterwards every noise gave rise to concern. This included the unexpected noise of my water bottle sloshing around in my rucksack, prompting me to spin round to locate the source of the noise. It was unreasoning (and embarrassing) alarm born of being alone, a long way from home in what was, for me, an alien environment. This was hardly Death Valley but Sabino Canyon was enough to raise my pulse for a while, and all the more enjoyable for it.

Tom Miller had arranged to meet me at one of his favourite restaurants, Mi Nidito ('My Little Nest'), on Tucson's south side. I'd been twisting myself in knots wondering how to approach the evening and in the end gave up twisting and decided just to chew the fat and see how things went.

Mi Nidito's main claim to fame is that Bill Clinton visited here - there are photos of his visit on every wall - in an attempt to woo the Hispanic vote after he'd been caught, as Tom put it, 'diddling the help'. It's a popular restaurant, more for its good food than its good taste in politicians, and a failure to make a reservation left us with 45 minutes to kill before we could eat. This gave Tom time to show me round the older part of Tucson, where the police, according to my host, are even more corrupt than in Tucson city proper.

Tom is originally from Washington DC but came out to the south west over 40 years ago decided to stay. He was active in the anti-war movement in the '60s and wrote extensively for the underground/alternative press and more recently for radical blog sites. He thinks the change of terminology from 'underground' to 'alternative' was significant, implying a shift from the political to the commercial and foreshadowing a retreat from the radical politics of the '60s.

He's been paying regular visits to Cuba since 1990, a time when the US embargo was still firmly in place and, after many bureaucratic hold-ups, married a Cuban woman. He's now sought out as a consultant by people wishing to visit Cuba (in 2011 still a potentially tricky proposition for American citizens) and has written a book, 'Trading With The Enemy', about his travels there. More recently he'd been involved in the campaign to oppose Proposition 1070, which introduced an Arizona state law allowing police officers to question, and if necessary detain, anyone who they have a 'reasonable suspicion' may not have the correct immigration documents. Put another way, it allows Arizona law officers to detain anyone they have a 'reasonable suspicion' may be Mexican. Even the Arizona Association of Chiefs of Police spoke out against the legislation.

A professional writer, Tom was keen to talk about his latest project, a book which will use Cervantes' 'Don Quixote' as a reference point for writing about the Spanish cities and regions visited by the book's hero. The conversation then bounced between the difficulties of writing for a living, Tom's ambiguous relationship with the tag 'travel writer', tastes in music (he's nothing if not obsessive, the owner of over 80 recordings of 'La Bamba' by various artists) to our shared fascination for the south west. We had a frustratingly short time to pursue all the strands of the conversation we'd opened up, but parted leaving open the possibility of meeting again in Bisbee where I was due to go in a few days' time.

To the south west of Tucson is the Kitt Peak National Observatory and I'd booked myself on one of the evening sky-gazing sessions there. Kitt Peak is almost 7,000 feet high and from the plain below the white oval housing of the telescopes (there are six of them) dotted along Kitt Peak's ridgetop looked tiny and impossibly difficult to reach. On the winding, ear-popping drive up to Kitt Peak I stopped a number of times to observe the Observatory as its real size unfolded.

The plan is for our group to watch the sunset through powerful binoculars and then to observe the night sky using binoculars and a couple of the observatory's telescopes. Our guide was Richard, an ex-train driver who became a volunteer guide (Americans use the word 'docent', a term I'd never heard before) at the Observatory before becoming a paid member of staff.

Richard used to drive night trains. Often his train would have to lay up overnight but Richard wasn't allowed to sleep as he had to guard the train. He tells us that during these layovers he taught himself the detailed geography of the night sky. Like all the guides I've come across in the States, Richard's subject knowledge is very impressive.

We watched the sun set over a mountain range to the west and Richard explained that at the precise moment that the lowest point of the sun's disc touched the horizon the sun had actually already set because, coincidentally, the earth's atmosphere 'bends' the light rays from the sun by an amount exactly equal to the diameter of the sun's disc. I'm a sucker for this stuff.

Looking through our powerful binoculars we then saw something quite amazing: just as the sun was about to disappear below the horizon a green aura appeared around the sun and then two sharp flashes of bright green, one either side of the sliver of sun that was still visible. Richard explained to us the cause of the flashes, something to do with refraction of the sun's light by the earth's atmosphere eliminating colours of the spectrum other than green. The explanation was largely lost on me, I'm no scientist. I can remember the beauty of those flashes though and that's good enough for me.

We then go over to the other side of the ridge to look at the eastern sky. There's a visible darkening of the clear blue sky running to a height of 15 to 20° above the eastern horizon. This is the earth's shadow, projected into space, which we can see in the evening sky. But that's not the whole story; the dark strip is the umbra, or darkest part, of the earth's shadow. Richard tells us to look up and there, directly above us, running roughly north east to south west, is a distinct line which marks the penumbra, or the lightest part of the earth's shadow. I can feel my jaw starting to drop and we haven't looked through the telescope yet.

To cut a long story short, highlights of the night sky are:

Through the telescope; seeing the rings of Saturn (and four of its moons) so perfectly that the planet looks like a little toy in the eye-piece; observing a ring nebula (an exploding star) and what is thought to be the largest galaxy yet discovered in the observable universe (it looks like candy floss in the eye-piece). The galaxy is 80 million light years away so the light which I observe through the telescope set off on its journey to me when dinosaurs walked the earth.

Through the binoculars the star Sirius dances in the sky emitting startlingly bright blue, green, white and red flashes of light. I keep coming back to it between telescope observations to watch another dance. We're shown how to spot an 'iridium flare' as the sun's light reflects off a cell phone communication satellite's solar panel. We observe a star which, viewed through the binoculars, turns out to be two stars locked in a gravitational embrace. Richard explains that two other stars we can see in the vicinity are also dual stars and that all six are being pulled together. At some point in the future it will end in tears for all of them.

We have to leave the Observatory with our car lights off as any white light near the telescopes can spoil the scientific observations being made. This feels like a tricky business but we're guided through it by the staff. We're warned about going too fast downhill as mountain lions and cows have been known to stray onto the steep mountain road that takes us back to level ground. A cow recently wrote off the car of a less-than-observant member of staff who took a blind corner too fast and found the cow staring into his windshield. Richard didn't say whether the cow had to be written off.

On my way back to Tucson I was stopped at a Border Patrol road block. We were very close to the Mexican border and the Border Patrol had been busy on this road all day. My sun-reddened tourist face bought me a free pass through the checkpoint but just ten minutes further up the road a fleet of prowl cars going in the opposite direction passed at speed with lights flashing and horns blaring. It's likely that some unfortunate had been unearthed at the road block I'd just passed through.

I saw a couple of bands in Tucson, one on purpose and one by accident, but both of them worth turning out for. Looking through the 'Tucson Weekly' a band called The Jive Bombers sounded like they'd be worth going to see. I went to the right place but unfortunately on the wrong night and it was The Ronstadts playing. As with the misfortune in New York this turned out to be no bad thing because the leaders of the band are Bill and Peter (or Petie) Rondstadt, cousins of the famous Linda, and singing clearly runs in the family. I later learned that the Ronstadts were a well-established Tucson family long before Linda became Linda.

The Ronstadts played extremely convincing Americana (I can't think of a better term), covering songs such as Chris Isaak's 'Wicked Game' and John Prine's 'Angel From Montgomery'. Bill Ronstadt in particular has a finely-honed tenor voice which he didn't get enough opportunities to show off.

I felt I owed it to the Jive Bombers to go and see them on the night they'd actually been booked to play and they turned out to be one of the more convincing blues band I'd seen. Driving home I tried to analyse why this might be, and decided that the difference sprung from the fact that they'd made a decent fist of swinging the blues. Played without feeling the blues can just lie on the floor until you feel like kicking it back to life. The Jive Bombers had moved their blues right along.

I wanted to walk in the desert while I was in Tucson and Saguaro National Park seemed to offer the best possibility of undertaking a walk that was within my capabilities given a knee, hip and cardio-vascular system that have all seen better days. The Sendero Esperanza ('Trail of Hope', appropriately enough) is about four miles long and far enough away, by unpaved road, from the park centre to get my heart beating again. Within a few minutes of leaving the car a sense of isolation set in which was both thrilling and worrying. The heat was distinctly desert-like even though I'd set off in the late afternoon, and after just ten minutes of walking there was no sign of any human intervention anywhere round me. I had to talk myself into keeping going by promising that I'd turn round at the first sight of a bleached skeleton.

Small lizards skittered across the trail and I caught sight of what I thought might be gophers. The park centre had given the now routine warnings about rattlesnakes and a leaflet had given instructions on what to do if you encountered a mountain lion. It said you had to make yourself as big as possible by raising your arms in the air – don't run away under any circumstances – and shout in a loud voice "Go away." I turned the page for the best approach if the mountain lion doesn't follow your instructions, but the leaflet fell silent at this point.

For shelter from the sun I stood under a huge, definitely old, possibly dying but still stately cactus which had lost all its spines except on one arm. My thoughts turned to the fate of the flaky yet unfortunate David Grundman and I took the precaution of not standing underneath the elderly saguaro's upturned arms. Contemplating the desert and my physical condition from the cactus's shade I decided against doing the full walk as the last stretch was a series of steep climbs that I knew would be a struggle. Instead I climbed just a little way up the next rise and was rewarded by a view of the desert that held me for an age. The desert stillness was everywhere.

Before taking my leave of Tucson my host, Els, became the joyous recipient of the third and final bottle of Henderson's and the ceremony was photographed by her partner for posterity. I'd enjoyed this desert city so much I'd stayed three nights longer than I'd planned.

TOMBSTONE, BISBEE & THE BORDER

I pulled into Tombstone at High Noon. I stepped into the sunlight and the heat hit me like a swinging saloon door. The flies gathered round as if they were pleased to see me. I pulled the brim of my hat low over my eyes and ambled up main street. A tall hombre sporting a grey handlebar moustache, packing twin pearl-handled guns that no real gunfighter would want to rely on in a showdown, eyed me up and down. I made my way over to him and fixed him with a Boot Hill stare.

"Where can a stranger get a drink around here?" I drawled. He pointed down main street, past the OK Corral and Big Nose Kate's Saloon. His finger was shaking. I smiled, touched the brim of my hat in appreciation and moved on. Grocery store clerks, waiters and dark-eyed senoritas from south of the border, venturing out into the midday heat to catch the action, held their breath. They were waiting for me to make my move.

I walked up to the bar. The bartender wiped beads of sweat from his upper lip. His eyes darted from side to side, refusing to meet mine. "What can I get you stranger?" he wheezed. "Gimme a root beer...in a dirty glass."

Hand-on-heart I pulled into Tombstone, Arizona, at 12 noon on the button. I strolled past the OK Corral and Big Nose Kate's Saloon and talked to a fancy-dan cowboy with a handlebar moustache and pearl-handled guns. He was paid to entertain the tourists. Oh, and I drank a root beer and very tasty it was too. The rest is made up, in case you're wondering.

I'd left Tucson heading south east towards the Arizona border towns of Tombstone, Benson, Bisbee and Douglas. My plan was to visit the border before travelling north into New Mexico and further north still to Monument Valley and the Grand Canyon. Tombstone was the first stop on the list. Arriving there at noon was good luck rather than good management and pleased me more than it should have done.

Is Tombstone a tourist trap? You bet, but enjoyable for all that. I even hung around in the boiling early afternoon sun to watch a couple of gunfights – one 'serious', one knockabout – both of them well-performed. And the kids there loved it. All of us did.

Bisbee is a scenic old mining town turned retiree-haven and baby-boomer artist colony in the Mule Mountains of southern Arizona. Five or six thousand people live here now. Buildings cling attractively to the sides of Tombstone Canyon and

Brewery Gulch. Bisbee reminded me strongly of Mediterranean coastal villages where all roads in from the mountains meet in the harbour area, which often serves as the village square too. The central area of Bisbee, the lowest part of town where the sea should start and the fishing boats should be moored, is a small car park.

Tom Miller had invited me to an open studio event hosted by two of his Bisbee friends, Boyd and Laurie. Boyd is a photographer, Laurie sketches and paints in water colours. Even after many years of living here it's obvious from their work that both are still in thrall to Arizona's light, textures, colours and geometry. I'd already begun to show symptoms of this same affliction.

I felt a little out of place as this was a gathering of local artists with much of the conversation revolving around current projects and, inevitably, insider artist politics. Nonetheless, southern manners and hospitality demanded that I be made welcome and comfortable. This duty was carried out admirably; everyone showed at least a polite interest in my journey. Others gave helpful suggestions on places to visit (and avoid) while I was here.

Discussion touched for a while on the topic of 'illegal' immigration, which has become permanent political background noise in the border area. This gathering was anything but antagonistic to Mexicans looking for a better standard of living in the States. I know some of them had campaigned against Arizona's anti-immigration statutes. But on the subject of immigration it's often easier for liberals and the left to say what we're against than what we're for, leaving discussions to tail off into resigned shrugs, which is what happened this afternoon in Bisbee.

> In the final analysis an open border is the only answer. But it will take a different sort of government arising out of a radically different society to bring that about. In the meantime, and until there is a wider fightback against free market policies, the right wing is able to set the terms of the immigration debate while the left fights tough but crucial rearguard actions.

As well as being a professional photographer, local tour guide, local historian and walking encyclopaedia, Tom's friend Boyd has at one time or another been a teacher, curator of the Bisbee Mining & Historical Museum, local elected official and Vietnam War draft resister. On a jeep tour with him I learned something of the social, economic, architectural and natural history of Bisbee.

The area around Bisbee was disputed territory between the US and Cochise's Apaches in the late 19th Century. The US Cavalry brought their horses to drink from a spring situated in what is now the heart of town and when two cavalry officers noticed the greenish tinge of copper sulphate in the hills the history of Bisbee changed forever. The officers filed claims on the land and sent off samples to the assay office. The samples contained high-grade copper. The finance needed to extract the valuable metal from the ground was provided by a venture capitalist from California named Judge DeWitt Bisbee, whose name and money became attached to the town.

Labour was provided by miners from around the world, including Cornish tin miners. The first miners brought under contract to Bisbee lived in tents; the mining companies took no responsibility for them other than paying their wages. Between working 10-12 hour shifts the contracted miners built their houses by hand in the canyons, using their own tools and dynamite bought from the company.

Bisbee boomed. It was a long way from here to anywhere else, the company was making large profits and were able to pay the miners well to keep the unions out. Prostitution boomed here too. Boyd pointed out tiny, single-storey houses with four doors and separate flights of steps up to each door. At the top of each flight of steps and behind each of the doors would have been a separate 'crib' where the miners were agreeably parted from their money.

The unions did establish a toehold here, but not for long. In 1917 a strike led by members of the Industrial Workers Of The World was broken by the Phelps Dodge Company (the biggest of the Bisbee mining companies) with help from the County Sheriff. Thirteen hundred men were illegally deported to New Mexico at gunpoint. Some of those deported had nothing to do with the strike, they were rounded up and shipped out simply because they weren't known to the sheriff's men. Wild West capitalism, red in tooth and claw.

Boyd, Laurie and Tom comfortably qualified for a bottle of Hendersons given the hospitality they showed to a complete stranger but supplies of the good stuff had been exhausted before I reached Bisbee. For their peace of mind I thought it best to leave without dropping this bombshell.

Bisbee is only six or seven miles from the US-Mexico border and the pedestrian border crossing at Naco. Road traffic crosses the border a little way east of the town itself. The road into Naco is long, straight and downhill offering a panoramic view of the small, unincorporated town surrounded by desert and overlooked by dark Mexican hills.

Naco was eerier than I could possibly have anticipated. Little or nothing moved there apart from a constant hot dusty breeze. The temperature was oppressive after the relative cool of elevated Bisbee. A dog slept in the middle of one of the main roads through town. Naco was every bit the desolate border town of the imagination, so much so that I was a little taken aback. I drove up to the fence dividing northern America from central America. English signs on this side, Spanish signs on the other. Flags competed for air space.

There were plenty of empty buildings and failed businesses on this side. There was a haulage yard still in operation, a grocery store and a car mechanic's workshop but every other building had been abandoned. The grocery store, just 20 yards from the border post, was painfully short on provisions, the freezer completely empty.

Only a thousand people live here but almost all of Naco's homes are surrounded by low wire mesh fences. The fences wouldn't keep anyone out of the house who was determined to get in but they reflect a state of readiness. Tension beneath the stillness.

The only person I saw walking around in the heat was an old man in straw hat, plaid shirt and jeans. He compulsively patrolled the same couple of blocks again and again. The heat didn't seem to bother him. I stayed much longer than was warranted by what there was to see or do, but hesitated to leave because I wasn't sure that I'd ever experience anything as alien as this again.

> That night I wrote in my notebook "Naco has the feel of a place that's been cursed". I found out later that the original town had been divided by the US and Mexican governments in the 1960s because of political tensions arising from drug and people smuggling. A crude border fence was built, the people separated but the problems have grown. Naco on the Mexican side of the border is known locally as 'Un pueblo chico, olvidadode Dios' (A small town, forgotten by God).

> The human spirit is hard to keep down though and every year, to celebrate the unity that their governments have stolen, the residents of Naco, Arizona, and Naco, Sonora, play a game of volleyball over the border fence. I don't know who keeps the ball.

I drove back up the long straight Naco Highway to Highway 92, watching the border recede in my overtaking mirror. At the T-junction where the Naco Highway meets Highway 92 I stopped at Jimmy's Hot Dog Company for a late breakfast. I ate 'Polish Sausage, Chicago-Style', a challenging green chilli pepper I really should have left alone and listened to slow blues on the juke box. When the place started to fill up the music switched to '50s pop and rock and roll.

I told the waitress about my trip down to Naco and she told me that I could have walked though the border crossing simply by showing my passport. No Border Patrol is likely to hound this westerner on the other side. For a while I considered returning but decided against. It would be like looking over the poor neighbour's back fence to see just what kind of mess their back yard is in. Instead I headed off for New Mexico, Silver City and the Gila Wilderness.

NEW MEXICO

I recorded these sights and signs travelling away from Naco:

On my way to Jimmy's Hot Dog Company I had passed a man standing in workday clothes by the side of the highway in 90 – 95°F heat. Not a hobo or a hitcher as far as I could tell, he was carrying a hand-written sign on a sheet of cardboard. The sign read "NEED WORK". I ate my breakfast and continued my journey about an hour and a half later. He was still there.

The US has a system called "Adopt A Highway". Companies, organisations, families and individuals can, for a fee, publicise themselves by having their name associated with a stretch of highway. A section of Highway 80 east of Douglas, Arizona, has been adopted by 'Cochise County Gay & Lesbian Alliance'. Out and proud in cowboy country.

Highway 80 was a lonely road once I'd passed through Douglas. Forty or fifty miles with few signs of life. The phone showed no signal here and my city boy nerves were tested as I thought of things that could go wrong. The land was flat and sun-bleached, almost lemon-coloured in places. Low hills erupted out of the flatland but were sucked back into the plain almost as quickly as they rose up.

A plume of smoke over to my left had been growing steadily larger, and occupying an increasingly large part of a cloudless sky, for about 45 minutes. The Coronado National Forest was ablaze, one of many summer fires to threaten Arizona and New Mexico this year. My route took me straight through the smoke which was heavy enough to blot out the sun for 10-15 minutes. This is a country of natural extremes. Tornadoes and floods have torn through parts of the mid-west and deep south and forest fires are breaking out across the south west.

The road to Gila Wilderness runs through Silver City in New Mexico. Like Bisbee it's an old mining town. This is the town where Billy The Kid was arrested and whose first marshal was 'Dangerous Dan' Tucker but today it's populated with art galleries, antique shops and artisan outlets.

Sidewalk kerbs are unusually high here because the town is prone to floods. In 1895 a deluge opened up a ditch 60 feet deep and 40 feet wide where Main Street used to be. According to the local museum the ditch has an interesting history of its own. Despite its size and notoriety, and the fact that it's spanned by a bridge, three people have found themselves at the bottom of it.

Elizabeth Powell was the first in 1904, then Averil Crebs disappeared over the edge together with his horse and carriage in 1914. His horse had been startled by a backfiring car. Richard Powel fell into the ditch in mysterious circumstances and is the only known fatality. The museum records that after a business trip to Las Cruces, and having been seen at various 'establishments' around town Mr Powel was swallowed up by the ditch at some point during his busy evening. The museum doesn't go into details about which establishments this solid citizen visited, but like me you may be speculating about how the evening could have left him so confused as to wind up at the foot of the biggest hole in town.

I searched the museum in vain for information about the 1951 strike at the Empire Zinc Mine in nearby Bayard. The strike became the subject of 'Salt Of The Earth', a largely forgotten film now regarded by some critics as one of the classic films of the twentieth century.

I'd first learned about the strike and the film's troubled production from Tom Miller's book, 'Jack Ruby's Kitchen Sink'. The book explains how, when miners were banned from picketing by a court ruling, their wives took over control of the picket line. The effect that this had on the strike, the miners' wives and their relationships with their husbands is one of the film's central themes.

Made in 1954 by Hollywood blacklisted film-makers and some of the men and women who took part in the strike, the film was effectively buried by the McCarthy witch-hunt and appeared in only a handful of cinemas after its release. You would leave Silver City museum completely ignorant of this important piece of New Mexico history.

(Out of copyright, the film can be viewed or downloaded legally and free from the Moving Image Archive or at publicdomainflicks.com.)

The hills crowded in on the valley road leading to Lake Roberts in the Gila Wilderness. This is a good place to get away from it all – one road into the wilderness, same road back out. Lake Roberts has 20 lodgings and one general store. You probably have more food in your house after a weekend shop than the Lake Roberts store had on the day I visited but Ian, who manages this store with no food in the middle of nowhere, is a drummer who says he stood in with Ike Turner's band in San Diego for a while. Music must be in the blood over here.

More forest fires around the site of Gila Native American cliff dwellings put that destination out of bounds but Lake Charles and the Gila River provided scenic and peaceful walking.

Further north on the road to Grants, New Mexico the highway was lined by a pygmy forest of saltbush, scrub oak, ponderosa pine, piñon and juniper lines the highway. At this point in my journey I was more or less following the Continental Divide. To the west of where I was driving river systems drain into the Pacific Ocean, to the east the Atlantic Ocean. In Grants I stayed for a couple of nights in the Sands Motel, made famous by its situation on Route 66 and the fact that Elvis and Priscilla Presley spent a night here on their honeymoon. The motel owner was good enough to let me look around the Presleys' surprisingly humble honeymoon suite, which has a copy of their marriage certificate on the wall. Who needs Gracelands?

To the south of Grants, along Highway 53, is an area of black cinder cones, lava caves and craters called El Malpais – 'the badlands' – by the first Spanish explorers. Even to the modern visitor, able to use well marked trails across the volcanic landscape, the lava fields still look distinctly threatening. A group of us climbed to the rim of one of the volcanoes which formed this forbidding landscape but in the course of many thousands of years much of the mouth of the volcano has been reclaimed by dust and small trees.

Further along the highway to the south west of Grants is El Morro, a sandstone mesa with a characteristic flat, wide summit and steep cliff sides some 200 feet high. 'Morro' is Spanish for a round hill or point of land, and is a place name I would encounter a number of times in a part of America which Spain had ruled for more than three centuries. The mesa is situated on an ancient east-west travel route and has a reliable waterhole at its base. A place of rest in an otherwise open and arid land, the bottom of the mesa is covered with more than a thousand inscriptions left by Spanish and Anglo travellers, and petroglyphs (symbolic rock engravings) left by the Pueblo Native Americans who lived in this part of the south west.

The inscriptions and petroglyphs fascinated me and I spent far too long trying to take decent photographs of them. The earliest inscription (the petroglyphs are centuries older than the inscriptions) is from 1605. It was left by Spanish adventurer, explorer and first governor of Spanish New Mexico, Don Juan de Oñate. Translated, the inscription reads, "Passed by here, the adelantado Don Juan de Oñate from the discovery of the sea of the south the 16th of April of 1605." His small group had undertaken what must have been an exhausting round trip as the 'sea of the south' is the Gulf of California, some 600 miles away.

At the top of the mesa, stone-built dwellings dating back to the 13th century have been partly excavated. It seems remarkable that anyone would choose to live up here – food and water are 200 feet down the cliff side – yet up to 800 people could have lived here at any one time. Two sides of the mesa afford a comprehensive view of the surrounding plain, a third side leads through a heavily wooded canyon to an accompanying mesa. The security provided by living up here may explain why these early Americans chose this lonely place, but it's only one possible explanation amongst many; climate change has been suggested, as has the religious beliefs of the Pueblo people. The fact is that nobody knows for sure why they came or why they left. El Morro mesa was only inhabited for about 75 years before being abandoned.

I clambered round the top of the mesa till the sun started to set, taking in the panoramic views of the plains below, trying to imagine the life these mysterious, tough, resourceful people must have led and making sure I avoid getting blown over the cliff side by the strong wind – no safety railings up here.

Before leaving Grants I experimented with 'Huevos Rancheros', a traditional Mexican breakfast that has been adopted across much of the south west. Two fried eggs came covered in chilli sauce, wrapped in a flour tortilla and accompanied by re-fried beans and fried potatoes. At 8.30 in the morning the chilli sauce grabbed the attention of my taste buds and made me uncomfortably aware of my mouth and stomach for the rest of the morning. Chilli sauce for breakfast makes an invigorating change from Bran Flakes, but the experiment couldn't be counted an unqualified success.

MONUMENT VALLEY &
THE GRAND CANYON

MONUMENT VALLEY & THE GRAND CANYON

I had a 230-mile drive north west from Grants to Bluff, Utah, last stop before Monument Valley and the Grand Canyon. The route to Bluff would take me due west initially through Gallup, New Mexico, probably the most memorable of the towns named in the song 'Route 66'. In deference to the famous song I pulled off the interstate to drive down Gallup's main street (one of the remaining stretches of Route 66) singing along to the Rolling Stones' version at the top of my voice with the windows open. I was safe enough – it was the Sunday before Memorial Day (a public holiday to remember the country's dead in its many foreign wars) so there were even fewer people walking round than usual.

North of Gallup the countryside started to take on a mottled look – green, brown and straw-coloured. The wind started to pick up, sending tumbleweed skittering across the road. Dust made the day dark, headlights went on and traffic slowed. Further north, enormous rocks and long flat-topped mesas, some of them covering a quarter of the horizon, rose up out of the high desert. Shiprock was particularly spectacular, rising immediately and massively from the plain to a height of 1500 feet. Further north still the land passed to a deeply ugly grey moonscape of rock, gullies and eroded mesas covered in small derricks and power cables. This devastated land has been granted to the Ute and Navajo nations.

I was very close to the 'Four Corners', the only part of the USA where four states (Utah, Arizona, New Mexico and Colorado) meet. I took a short diversion to the tourist spot which marks the precise point of convergence and succumbed to the temptation to walk round four states in ten seconds and have my circumnavigation filmed for posterity.

Driving towards the town of Bluff trees cluster protectively round the San Juan river, the deep green standing in sharp contrast to the stunning red (closer to rose pink) sandstone that now dominates the landscape. Bluff is a handsome, tiny tourist town surrounded by – you guessed it – bluffs. When I arrived the wind had whipped up a pink-grey dust cloud that closed off visibility beyond 30-40 metres.

Bluff is dominated by Twin Rocks, a couple of towers carved by wind and water which resemble – there's no way round this really – a pair of giant phalluses standing side by side. An unfortunate natural phenomenon in a town founded by Mormons and just the first of many incredible natural formations carved by wind, water and time that I was to see in the next few days.

After a single night in Bluff I started out the next day at 7.15am. A thick band of cloud to the east hid the sun for a while but thankfully the wind had stalled overnight and visibility was good. It was worth the effort of an early start. I had the road to myself and within 10-15 minutes of driving south west from Bluff I came upon Mexican Hat, a flying saucer-shaped rock 60 feet wide and 12 feet thick perched ever-so precariously on a column of sandstone like a plate on a stick. If you're thinking of visiting I should go soon, it didn't look too stable.

A little further down the road I stopped the car to take in the cliffs, buttes and mesas that surrounded me; I was filming a range of cliffs and heard what could only have been an animal scream coming from the direction I was filming. The sound reminded me that as much as I was feeling completely alone (I could see for miles without any signs of life) this beautiful but inhospitable countryside teems with life.

This early-morning encounter was an overture to the main theme provided by the Navajo Tribal Park and Monument Valley. I'd heard from a few people of the beauty of the valley but in truth nothing could prepare you for the first view of the colossal buttes, some as high as 1000 feet, which are scattered below the park's main veranda. It's not hard to understand how this became a sacred place. The buttes look as if they could have been carved and thrown down to earth by an idle deity. Two formations, the mittens, are almost perfect mirror images of each other. It seems impossible they could have been caused by natural processes alone.

After the viewing platforms and the visitor centre I drove down amongst the behemoths of the valley bottom, past elephant rock and the three sisters. Progress is slow because of the unevenness of the trail. The Navajo nation – presumably for a combination of commercial and spiritual reasons – have kept the valley road unpaved. I couldn't afford the full Navajo-led jeep tour at this stage of the trip and didn't want to expose my little Nissan's tyres to an arduous 17 mile journey on rocky roads so my excursion into the depths of the valley was a short but breathtaking one.

I had a 150 mile journey to the north rim of the Grand Canyon ahead of me, working my way south west, up through the spectacular high country of the Navajo reservation before turning north west and on to Highway 98. The rugged northern Arizona terrain doesn't tolerate straight roads and I would be forced to describe a sizeable horseshoe-shaped arc towards Page – a small town founded to house workers constructing the nearby Glen Canyon Dam – and then south to Jacob's Lake, my final destination for the day.

About 30 miles after Page the road, travelling steeply uphill, burrowed through a notch in the cliffs and on the downhill stretch the most remarkable panorama opened up. I'd arrived at Vermilion Cliffs, a place which is marked on road maps but not mentioned in any of the guide books I'd read before making the trip. The cliffs, of the deepest red sandstone and 3000 feet in height, surround a flat green valley, maybe 30 or 40 miles wide, to the north and south. I arrived in the late afternoon, the sun picking out sharp details on the cliff's surfaces. The highway took me down the elongated north cliffs, across the valley floor and up through the south cliffs.

My notebook, written up that evening, reads, "scale of what lies before me is terrifyingly beautiful. No words or photographs could adequately describe. Close to tears on two or three occasions at its beauty."

After a day unlike any other I'd experienced I slept at the Jacob's Lake Inn, around 40 miles north of the Grand Canyon north rim. Although it was the end of May, at an elevation of almost 8000 feet, the evening and morning hours were decidedly chilly. Clumps of snow stuck to the earth in shady areas between the aspen and firs. In winter, this part of northern Arizona can be covered in 10 feet of snow. The contrast with yesterday's hot and arid journey couldn't have been starker. Apart from the areas recovering from a recent fire the road is surrounded by meadows and lush forests.

The next day I arrived at the edge of the canyon. Carved by the Colorado river and its tributaries, the overwhelming sense here is one of time rather than space, deep time that can sculpt the fins, spires, towers and cliffs that fill this gash in the earth. And the colours are dizzying; layer after layer of exposed rock - ochre, pink, cream and the deep green of the pinyon and ponderosa pines covering the sides of the canyon.

On foot I followed a trail which runs parallel to the rim for about a mile and a half. Along the way there was a wooden bench overlooking the canyon and only set back slightly from the rim. "Roll up, roll up ladies and gentlemen, look back 2 billion years into geological time. Best seat in the house." A park bench like you've never experienced in your life.

> *The beauty testifies to natural processes but inspires unnatural thoughts. What would it be like to dive from the rim? What sights you'd see on the way down! What a way to go! A primitive urge to fly and to die spectacularly.*

Literature at the visitor centre tells of 600 recorded fatalities here and it's not hard to see why. Where the rim falls sheer away I tried to get as close to the edge as possible to see straight down but I'm protected by inbuilt caution. Two feet is as close as I dare get. Others may not have been as cautious. Dying wouldn't be so difficult here.

At different points in my walk I spotted a Kaibab squirrel (blood red body and stark white tail – an endangered species endemic to the north rim), a woodpecker and a family of gophers. A happy day; one when it felt good to be alive.

I was prompted to think about death again the following day while riding a mule called Fred into the canyon. The first 10-15 minutes were truly and genuinely terrifying. Fred was taller than I'd imagined, about 5 feet to the shoulders, so I was further away from the ground than I was comfortable with. The winding path into the canyon was very narrow, in places one side of the path fell away steeply unveiling a drop of many hundreds of feet. Fred showed altogether too much interest in eating the vegetation growing on the potentially fatal side of the path, giving me an unanticipated but clear view of our fate should he get spooked and lose his footing.

After a while terror was replaced by an uncomfortable but acceptable level of unease, a degree of trust in Fred's burro genes and an appreciation of the fact that we were inside the Grand Canyon, about a third of the way down, a place on the earth I never imagined I'd be.

Later, at the suggestion of Ron, one of the trail leaders who took us down into the canyon, I visited Point Imperial to the east of the visitor centre before leaving for Flagstaff. The canyon is much wider here and I could see the San Francisco mountains of northern Arizona clearly on the other side. Ron has lived around, and worked in, the Grand Canyon for over 40 years and explained that the breathtaking, magisterial landscape we'd been exploring by mule is in fact a mere side canyon running north from the main east-west artery.

Earlier in the visit I'd copied down the words of Clarence Dutton, a 19th century geologist so moved by his experience of working in the Grand Canyon that he wrote this unscientific but insightful summary of its emotional impact,

> *"Dimension means nothing to the senses and all we are left with is a troubled sense of immensity."*

ROUTE 66 TO CALIFORNIA

As the crow flies it's a relatively short distance from the Grand Canyon's north rim to Flagstaff, Arizona, but the road lay-out and the barrier presented by the eastern section of the canyon itself dictated a drive of over 200 miles back through Bitter Springs, Marble Canyon, a return journey through the dream-like valley surrounded by Vermilion Cliffs, looping south again via Highway 89 to Flagstaff, putting me back on Interstate 40 and, more interestingly, Route 66.

For the music fan, evocatively-named towns stud this famous east-west route like jewels on a bracelet – Holbrook, Winslow, Kingman, Barstow. Route 66 and the interstate highway run close to, and parallel with, the rail track for a long stretch, making these towns look superficially similar; their main streets follow the original configuration of Route 66 while rail tracks and interstate run on the south side of town.

I'd expected Flagstaff to be an industrial town, but the proximity of the University of Northern Arizona, the outdoor activities provided by the San Francisco mountains and the fact that this is a jumping-off point for the more popular south rim of the Grand Canyon have led to education and tourism replacing lumber and ranching as the main economic activities.

Setting out from Flagstaff I visited the nearby Walnut Canyon National Monument. Walnut Creek, a tributary of the Little Colorado river, has cut a small canyon here 20 miles long, 350 feet deep and a quarter of a mile wide. Erosion has created substantial overhangs within the canyon which were inhabited by native Americans for something like 800 years until, as at El Morro in New Mexico, the people mysteriously abandoned the dwellings they'd created and moved on.

Again the impression is of a hardy and adaptable people. The dwellings have the remains of masonry walls which gave shelter (we're still at an elevation of almost 7,000 feet and winters here can be hard) and divided the space under the overhangs into family units. These early Americans fed themselves by farming and hunting around the rim of the canyon, the Little Colorado river and winter snow-melt provided the water.

> *At this stage of the trip the image I'd carried, fostered by TV and film, that all Native Americans drifted across the western plains living in tepees had been properly rubbished. I'd visited permanent, constructed settlements in the low hills of Georgia, on a spectacular mesa plateau in New Mexico and built into the walls of a canyon in Arizona.*

Leaving Flagstaff I followed the I-40 west for 30 miles before turning off to follow Route 66 on a loop to the north which brought me back on to the interstate 60 miles further west at Kingman.

My first stop on this stretch of the road was Seligman which, despite all the shops selling souvenirs and memorabilia to Route 66 buffs, had the authentic and attractive feel of a desert town. In Angel and Vilma Degadillo's Gift Shop I was asked, not for the first time, if I was Scottish. My standard reply (that I'm from the north of England, by US standards not too far from Scotland) prompted an enquiry from Vilma as to whether or not I know Billy Connolly. I confirmed that Billy and myself aren't personally acquainted, though under close questioning I turned out to be better informed about the Big Yin's life story than I'd expected.

Clearly impressed, Vilma told me that Connolly, making a documentary about Route 66, passed through Seligman just a few weeks before and she showed me a photograph of the whole family with the man himself posing in the middle. I considered asking them if they wanted to have their photograph taken with me as well but, fearing rejection, thought better of it. So I missed out on the chance to have my photograph taken with someone who'd had their photograph taken with Billy Connolly. Such opportunities come rarely in life.

> For the next 60 or 70 miles the 'mother road' ran parallel to the railroad line which pleased me no end. So quiet is the road and so infrequent the trains that I can stand on the line to take a photograph of the tracks running off to the horizon. Emptiness, the addictive signature tune of the south west, surrounds me.

The highlight of my overnight stay in Kingman was a vintage car show – what more fitting tribute to Route 66? A little oddly, the centrepiece of the show was an attempt to blow up the engine of a clapped-out car by running it at catastrophically high revs. But this banger was a tough old beast and after 20 minutes the engine was still screaming its complaints to the crowd. I drifted away thinking about a bullfight: the poor old car might put up a good fight but it couldn't win.

There was a huge billboard at the side of the main road through Kingman prophesying "Judgement day" on May 21st. Just to make sure you got the picture a vivid yellow sticker announced categorically, and a little threateningly (we're talking about the end of the world here) that "The Bible Guarantees It". The confident tone of the billboard was undermined a little by the fact that I was taking a photograph of it on 5th June. I couldn't really understand why the billboard was still up unless the hire terms had forced the sponsors (familyradio.com) to take the advertising space for a minimum period of time. With Armageddon approaching I guess the evangelists at familyradio.com must have been prepared to take the financial hit to get the message out.

East of Kingman, still on Route 66, changes in the colours and vegetation of the countryside suggested that I'd arrived at the eastern edge of the Mojave desert. The Joshua tree is the main vegetation here, the road narrowed, climbed and switchbacked through arid steep low hills.

It was a bit of a shock to realise that this had been the main route from the Midwest to the west coast until the interstate was built. It's a small, lonely, winding road through desolate farmland and steep hillsides at this point. I thought about the Okies making their way from the dustbowl that the Midwest had become in the Great Depression. Having almost reached the promised land of California this stretch of the mother road up and over Sitgreaves Pass – 100°F plus today and still not the height of summer – must have been heartbreaking.

I arrived in Oatman next, which is miles from anywhere. Like Tombstone, this is an old mining town which had become a semi-ghost town until it was rescued by the tourist trade. Route 66, and the baby boomer interest in all things rock and roll, had saved Oatman. As in Tombstone, Old West characters roam the streets here, spurs jangling, everyone's 'pardner'. Donkeys roam the streets here too. Semi-wild, they come into town during the day, pester tourists for snacks, shit on Main Street (the smell's not unpleasant) and at night they go back to the shelter of spent mine workings in the nearby hills.

The centrepiece of town is the Oatman Hotel. The downstairs rooms of the hotel are covered from floor to ceiling with thousands of dollar bills signed by visitors and stapled to the walls. A fire here would be a financial disaster for more reasons than one. If you ever visit the Oatman Hotel my signed dollar bill is near the entrance, on the left-hand side.

> *Fifteen to twenty miles west of Oatman Route 66 joins Highway 95 and the long, downhill run into Needles. There was no highway sign to confirm it, no bells and whistles, but this was a bit of a blue-ribbon moment in terms of the trip. After more than two months of travelling cross-country I'd crossed the state line into California.*

THE ROAD GOES ON FOREVER

HISTORIC ROUTE 66

YAVAPAI COUNTY

ROOKTON RD

NEEDLES & THE DESERT

First impressions of Needles are of a scruffy oasis town, though I think Needles is trying to be a resort. It boasts the usual motels, a marina of sorts built into the banks of the Colorado river which runs along the edge of town, and a small golf course. But Needles' strong suit is its proximity to the Mojave desert. There's keen local competition for the tourist dollar from Laughlin, a sub-Las Vegas gambling centre, and Bullhead City on the shores of Lake Mohave but Needles is OK by me. Situated in the wide Mohave Valley, there's lots of elbow room here. And it's hot – really, really hot.

The cold, fast-flowing river is Needles' saving grace and I took to the water a couple of times during my stay. This was the same water that had flowed through the Grand Canyon and I was, I happily imagined, swimming amongst eroded bits of the canyon floor which the river was carrying on its long journey down to the Gulf of California.

> *Not that you'd say the river is a particularly restful place at this point in its journey. Speedboats and jet-skis scream out of the marina and down the Colorado at lightning speed, howling their way back just a few minutes later. It's an aquatic drag-racing strip.*

My plan was to take a couple of trips into the desert using Needles as my base. The I-40 runs directly west from here along the southern border of the Mojave National Preserve. After a night's rest I drove 40 miles or so west and turned off into the desert heading for a couple of recreation sites, Hole-In-the-Wall and Mitchell Caverns, but a few miles into the desert were signs telling that Mitchell Caverns was closed. What to do? The caverns are about 10 miles into the desert along a road that no-one but me seemed to be using. If the caverns were closed, would Hole-In-the-Wall be open? The signs didn't say.

I carried on a little further, concern eating me up. After taking into account the pitiful supply of water I'd brought, the lack of a signal on my phone and the fact that I'd not seen another car since I turned off the interstate highway, my resolve failed and I doubled back.

> *City Boy 0 – Desert 1. No contest.*

I retreated back to the I-40, made my way back east for a few miles and then back into the National Preserve along a stretch of Route 66 leading to Goffs and my first ghost town. One building, the old Goffs General Store, is still standing – just – by a desert crossroads. The General Store used to have two-storeys but the second storey has collapsed for the most part, leaving only a façade on two sides. A storage tower built into a corner of the store is still standing.

When the interstate overtook Route 66 it seems that time ran out for Goffs. It's still possible to sense the spirit of the place though, in the desert light and the wind that blows through the General Store's broken windows. I'd been so keen to visit a ghost town and here I'd stumbled across Goffs completely by accident. So much for travel planning.

Still heading east from Goffs I followed the old Santa Fe rail track that runs parallel to the road through this part of the Mojave. I chased and overtook a freight train while a biker in shades and bandana chased and overtook me. Shades of Easy Rider. Him that is, not me. But in my head at least this road movie scene played out well for a few minutes. The train and the biker may have been the stars but I enjoyed my bit part.

Travelling east on this stretch of Route 66 ends at the intersection with Highway 95 which runs north to south. I could have turned right and returned to Needles or turned left to go to Laughlin on the southern tip of Nevada. Laughlin won. Laughlin always wins in the end because it has all the roulette wheels, crap tables and slot machines. In the 1960s a property developer called Don Laughlin bought a riverside motel building in this bit of the Nevada desert and turned it into the Riverside Resort Hotel And Casino. More casinos followed until, after Las Vegas and Reno, Laughlin (yes, they named the town after him) has now become the third biggest gambling centre in the state. It's an oddity that while Detroit mob figures have been associated with Laughlin's casino boom for years the town has one of the lowest crime rates in the country. Which raises the awkward question of whether the cops or the mob have the most effective methods for keeping people in line.

Casino Drive, Laughlin's main street, is surrounded by the huge, crass hotels and gambling houses that are Laughlin's only raison d'etre. The Riverside, the Colorado Belle – constructed to resemble a paddle steamer complete with fake paddle wheels and smokestacks – and the Tropicana Express. Apart from the odd, small shopping mall and 'Subway' fast-food outlet there's nothing that you would identify with a normal town centre. Laughlin has been ruthlessly put together to serve the single purpose it was designed for. A couple of hours here was enough. My day had come all unravelled, I'd started by seeking out the sparse loneliness of a California desert but ended up in the alienated loneliness of a Nevada gambling town.

On my way back to Needles I stopped on the California-Nevada border. Another car pulled up at the same time. The three passengers in it clearly had the same purpose as me, to photograph themselves next to the state border signs. As a lone traveller it was a lucky stroke for me as we were able to swap cameras and photograph each other. Performing this tourist ritual I fell into a long conversation with Billy Pebbles, a gentle soul with a soft Tennessee accent. Billy had worked for the massive DuPont Company but had happily retired 23 years ago at the age of 53. "Never been anywhere before I retired," he told me, but he'd got the travel bug now alright and had journeyed all across the south west during his retirement years, a long way from his native state.

We talked pleasantly about this and that for 20 minutes or so until the time seemed right to go our separate ways. But Billy was anxious to tell me one more thing - that he was a Jehovah's Witness - and to explain to me as concisely as he could given the circumstances of our meeting, the nature of his faith. I imagine it must be second nature for a proselytiser like Billy to try and show people the way whenever and wherever he can. He told me that he'd been knocking on doors all his life, had some of them slammed in his face, been called bad names and even been spit on. Having warmed to Billy during our conversation I became unreasonably angry at the people who would do this to him.

We shook hands four or five times preparing to say goodbye but on each occasion we found something else to talk about. Eventually Billy called over his travelling companions, his wife and her cousin (they'd been sitting in the car, patiently sweating while we talked) and introduced them to me. As I'd freely admitted my convinced atheism to Billy earlier in our conversation I took this as a great compliment. I parted from this quiet American happy at the coincidence that had brought us together on the California-Nevada border.

This was my only full day in Needles, I'd planned to move on to Barstow, 160 miles away at the other end of the Mojave, the following day. But, still stinging from the timorous end to my desert trip the day before I decided to do a little research, found out that Hole-In-The–Wall was still open and determined on making an early start and doing my small desert exploration a day late, on the way to Barstow.

> *Turning off the interstate the following morning I drove the 20 miles or so to Hole-In-the-Wall, sharing the road with just one car which was coming in the opposite direction. I'd found a walk that would take me through Banshee Canyon, so-called because of the howling noise the canyon makes when the wind blows through it.*

Five minutes into the walk I felt the same lonely, lovely stillness I'd experienced in the Sonora desert outside Tucson. A complete, almost mystical, stillness. Just me, a few small lizards cutting across the trail, the occasional rustling in the brush and the breeze investigating the undergrowth.

> *The desert didn't care that I was here, it didn't care if I left. It didn't care if I died here. It's implacable. Like the rest of the natural world of course, but the difference is that here you feel the implacability. It's tangible, it vibrates in the air.*

Implacable and beautiful; an unlikely and colourful assortment of wild flowers, brush and cacti covers the desert floor. The dark red body of a bulbous cactus (a barrel cactus, I discovered later) stood out. It was completely unexpected, this profligacy of life here.

I worked my way round a low ridge until I reached the mouth of a narrow canyon that I would part-walk and part-climb. I shouted a greeting into the canyon and the pitted volcanic rock threw it back. I felt the need to shout the names of my family; the canyon returned those to me too. It hit me that I'd been away from home a long time.

The walk up through the canyon was short and a little testing – for me at least – in a couple of places, but steel rings driven into the rock at steep points were there to aid the less-than-completely-fit hiker. Emerging from the canyon I met my first human being out here but we exchanged nothing more than brief 'hellos' before parting again.

There was a choice now; drive deeper into the Mojave, looping my way anti-clockwise on unpaved tracks to rejoin the interstate 40 miles further west, or make my way back the way I had come. But really it was no contest. The desert pulled me in, tempting me to ignore signs telling me that only 4-wheel drive vehicles should venture any further. My little Nissan Versa shuddered and bounced on the rough surface, forcing me to weave from one side of the track to the other to avoid the worst of the bumps, holes and sharp stones.

The reward was worth the risk. I drove through a jungle of joshua trees. The sharp leaves of beaked yuccas shimmered a memorable, vivid green against dark hills. I was so alone and so confident that I wouldn't be sharing the track with anyone else I filmed through the windscreen as I drove, fittingly accompanied by Ry Cooder and Little Feat's desert road music.

As I turned left over rail tracks to make the final downhill run to Kelso Depot – one of the few inhabited places in the Mojave – there was another entirely unexpected sight. Kelso Dunes, a glowing yellow mound of sand 600 feet high. Early western travellers must have imagined they'd found El Dorado when they first laid eyes on these dunes; from a distance it looks for all the world like a mountain of gold.

The sand grains that make up the 45 square miles of Kelso Dunes are blown by prevailing winds from the Mojave River and from the Soda Lake basin north west of the dunes and deposited here as the wind stalls and flips back on itself. It's possible to climb the dunes but not for me, not today. I have to be content with walking to the foot of the dunes, an imposing sight close up, and whispering to them "Next time... maybe" before starting the 100 mile drive to Barstow.

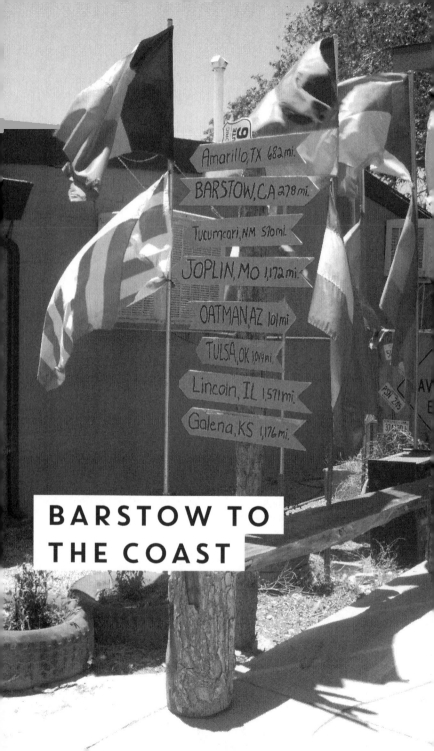

BARSTOW TO THE COAST

"We were somewhere around Barstow on the edge of the desert when the drugs began to take hold. I remember saying something like 'I feel a bit lightheaded; maybe you should drive . . .' And suddenly there was a terrible roar all around us and the sky was full of what looked like huge bats, all swooping and screeching and diving around the car, which was going about a hundred miles an hour with the top down to Las Vegas. And a voice was screaming, 'Holy Jesus! What are these goddamn animals?'"

The opening lines to 'Fear And Loathing In Las Vegas', one of the books which has contributed to the mystique of the western desert lands. Even as I was reading the book in the mid-1970s I knew that I would never have Hunter S. Thompson's wildness, and admired and shunned it in equal measure. I was completely absorbed by his flashy words for a while, then forgot them, though the spirit of his writing lingers.

Unfortunately Barstow was only an overnight stay for me as I was heading for the coast the next day. Around the motel pool I chatted to Nancy, a peripatetic nurse from Phoenix, Arizona. Nancy couldn't find work in Phoenix so she was following the work and had just got hired in Barstow. She was working on short-term contracts – three months at a stretch – wherever she could get them. Usually seven straight 12-hour shifts and then seven days off, which is when she could go back to visit her family. It's not what she wanted she told me, but it's a way of life they've had to get used to.

Nancy is far from poor and wouldn't want anyone's sympathy, but it's symptomatic of the current dominance of capital over labour here that even someone with a professional health qualification and years of experience in the field has to get on her bike to find work which isn't guaranteed beyond a few weeks. Put simply, the American labour market is a Tory Chancellor's wet dream.

The next day's drive was uneventful until I passed to the west of San Bernadino, heading towards the San Gabriel mountains. I could see the peaks of the San Gabriels running across the horizon and although there was clear blue sky overhead, I could see clouds at the foot of the mountains further down the road. The world seemed to have turned upside down, and it was such an unusual sight that I began to take photographs through the windscreen as I was driving.

At the foot of the mountains I drove into thick cloud and the road dropped away in a long, steep, curving downhill run. There were lots of warning signs with dramatic exclamation marks, run-off slip roads in case our brakes failed, limited visibility – heart-racing stuff. Within a couple of minutes I had to turn the car's air conditioning off and wind the windows up tight. While driving through the clouds the temperature had dropped 25-30°F.

This was my first taste of California 'June gloom'. Banks of marine cloud form over a still-cold Pacific and drift across the coast. On a bad day like today the cloud can stretch 40-50 miles inland, even in the southern part of the state. The Beach Boys never wrote a song about June gloom.

And the gloom isn't all you have to watch out for here. I was driving across the north east suburbs of Los Angeles, passing turn-offs with glamorous names – Pasadena, Burbank, San Fernando – but the drive itself was far from glamorous. The traffic here is heavier, faster and more aggressive than anywhere else on the trip.

On US freeways and interstates you can pass on the left or the right, which hadn't been a problem till now, but skirting round Los Angeles it would have been useful to have three eyes; one on the car in front and one fixed on either overtaking mirror. Sticking to the inside lane doesn't help that much either – traffic was streaming in from slip roads on my right almost constantly. I longed for the endless, lonely roads of Arizona and New Mexico. The torture lasted until I was clear of the greater L.A. area and heading north-west towards the coastal town of Ventura.

I arrived in Ventura in the late afternoon. A quick check-in and turn around and I was back out to do another 25 miles north along the coast to Santa Barbara. It would have been much too exclusive a place for me to stay in, but on this night the Santa Barbara Bowl was hosting a re-union concert by Buffalo Springfield, a favourite band from the '60s, and I'd got a ticket. The band exploded after a couple of years under the huge centrifugal force exerted by the musical egos of band members Neil Young and Steve Stills, but the old sparring partners had buried the hatchet and were doing a short tour with original band member Richie Furay and a couple of pals from the old days.

The Santa Barbara Bowl is an outdoor arena, it was an evening concert and distinctly cold. Who'd have thought it in California? I had to dash half a mile to the thrift (charity) shop to pick up an extra layer of clothing. I shelled out $10 for an ill-fitting, slightly foxed second-hand top here in swanky Santa Barbara and hoped that the charity would use my money wisely.

My seat was just three or four rows from the back of The Bowl, so I was hardly within touching distance of my adolescent heroes, but my ticket had bought me a panoramic view of Santa Barbara bay over to the right – palm trees, yachts, setting sun, the works. Dream-time California. Unfortunately, at the express instructions of the ex-hippies in the band all cameras had to be checked in at the gate, so you'll have to take my word for it. Bloody rock stars.

The audience was, for the most part, the Woodstock generation reconvened. Lots of hugging, hand-shaking and bead rattling. These baby boomers are pretty well-heeled these days – top-of-the-range boots, bandanas and denim - but my immediate neighbours were skater kids, reeking of booze and ganga, very friendly and talkative. I've never been called 'dude' so many times in my life.

The band played really well. They couldn't turn the volume right up though – the Bowl is in the sort of residential area that must have a lot of pull at City Hall. The vocals were a little shaky at times, but the occasion triumphed over any flaws in the performance. If The Beatles had re-formed to play tracks from Revolver and Rubber Soul nobody would have carped over a few bum notes - that's how I looked at it anyway.

In 2000 Neil Young wrote the gorgeously wistful track 'Buffalo Springfield Again' for his solo album 'Silver And Gold'; "Used to play in a rock and roll band, But they broke up... Maybe now we can show the world what we got. But I'd just like to play for the fun we had. Buffalo Springfield again." Well, Neil had got his wish and here he was making the most of it, bouncing around the stage like a puppy dog. It was worth the admission just to watch the old curmudgeon enjoying himself so much. A night to remember and yes, I did buy a T-shirt.

"I heard an old song playing on the radio...."

VENTURA &
ST LUIS OBISPO

I'd planned to spend a couple of days in Ventura, which had looked unprepossessing from the highway but in fact turned out to be very much how I'd imagined small town California. Low-rise and genteel. In the downtown area there are high quality thrift shops, coffee houses, pasta bars, diners and swish clothes shops on Ventura's main street. The thoroughfare runs parallel to the shore line and is called, rather imaginatively, Main Street.

California Street runs across Main Street and down to the Pacific Ocean. I walked down California Street on my first morning for my first sight of the Pacific Ocean, a stretch of water I genuinely thought I'd never see. On this gloomy day the Pacific was disappointingly brown, muddy and turbulent. I promenaded along Ventura's fine old-fashioned wooden pier which stretches a quarter of a mile out to sea. For decades the pier was a mooring/unloading point for commercial trawlers but today it's a recreational area; middle-aged couples, anglers and hooded youngsters on stunt bikes mix unselfconsciously. On the edge of the beach below the promenade, families of ground squirrels clambered around on rocks that they've colonised for as long as anyone here can remember.

Back in town I was drawn like a magnet to the 'Bank Of Books' at the top end of East Main Street. It's colossal – two huge floors stuffed with second-hand books. Clarey is the owner and he looks like an elderly Jimmy Durante. He's a big, engaging man and we talked for quite a while. He told me that they have two other outlets and a warehouse holding two million books. Anything I want they can get – first editions, rarities, out-of-prints, you name it. It's a line I heard him repeat a few times to different customers but that's fine. What intrigues me is how they dig out the books that they're asked for. Do they have a classification system and a muscular computer to help out? Nope says Clarey, they look in what seems to be the most likely section and stumble about till they find the book in question. Which is how any self-respecting second hand book shop should be run.

Stumbling aimlessly about works for me today. Browsing in the 'South West USA' section I found 'Desert Solitaire: A Year In The Wilderness' by Edward Abbey, an author I'd been introduced to by reading Tom Miller's book. Abbey was a radical environmental activist who took a job with the National Parks Service to get as close to the stony beauty of his beloved Utah – and as far away from human beings – as possible. Abbey's eco-warrior politics verge on the nihilistic but his love of this bit of America is palpable and he writes about it simply and elegantly. I recommend 'Desert Solitaire' to anyone with an interest in finding out more about the south west.

My next stay for a couple of days would be Santa Maria, which is about 80 miles north and inland from Ventura. Santa Maria is a lovely name for a fairly nondescript town, but it's convenient for the central California coast and for crossing the Sierras, which I was planning to do in a couple of days' time.

Driving between coastal towns the contrast with Arizona couldn't be starker; no red sandstone here but neat shades of green. This is wine country. The stretch of coast to the west of Santa Maria is unremarkable. A string of tourist towns (Pismo Beach, Avila Beach, Grover Beach) all offer variations on the same theme; shops, cafes, tattoo parlours and more shops. Fish and chips is popular here, though there's strong competition from clam chowder and cotton candy (candy floss to me and you). There was a fresh sea breeze on the day I visited, briskly reminiscent of Skegness in March, which forced even the hardiest of families to shelter in hoodies and behind wind breaks.

Some people, though, were unaccountably in swimwear. To me it felt 60°F at best and I wondered whether it was their nervous systems that were malfunctioning or mine. Still, I took the chance to paddle in the Pacific, a first, and to observe a charming, if rather wind-blown, California beach wedding.

I ate tea at a Mexican restaurant in Grover Beach; a bowl of fish broth that had the lot – octopus, squid, carrots, celery, cabbage, shrimp and an enormous crab claw that looked as if it could crawl out of the bowl and stir my coffee. Recognising my bewilderment the helpful young Californian behind the counter came to my aid, instructing me in the best way to subdue and dismantle the claw and extract its delicious meat.

An older Latino comes in and cheerfully demands chips and beer; "Right. now for the beer," he explains. "Just got off work". He and the waiter fall into conversation over the counter. Like many Americans the young waiter is holding down two jobs. During the week he's training as a dental technician and tells the older worker that the high-flyers in his group can do 150 dental impressions in a day. He's up to 120 and he's only been there a short while, he enthuses.

The older worker listens politely, takes the first taste of his beer and, better versed in the dynamics of the system, dispenses some sage advice; "Listen, don't do 150," he warns. "You could make a quarter million for the company in a day and all they're gonna say to you is, 'What you gonna do for me tomorrow…?'." "Amen to that, brother," my inner voice applauds as I wrestle with the claw.

I drove into the San Rafael mountains the following day. These aren't the rocky, forbidding hills of the 'four corners'; softer climatic conditions make for more accommodating green hillsides which fold gently into each other. Inviting they may be but it proves impossible to consummate the relationship. There's no help here for the would-be hiker, no trailheads, no notices, nothing, it was like driving round a large, private estate. The one ranger station I came across was long-deserted, the brochure bin full of bird feathers and spiders. it was all deeply frustrating. On the return journey I turned north onto route 101 and called into Nipomo to stretch my legs. This was small-town California; quiet, flat, dusty, middle-class. In Neeta's café a bluebird landed on a rail just two feet away from where I was sitting, stared at me for a long time (hoping for sandwich crumbs I suspect) and, single-handedly, rescued my day.

On Sunday afternoon I strolled through San Luis Obispo, 'The Happiest City in America' according to its own website. Attractive, tree-lined streets criss-crossed a small, well-demarcated town centre. Just north of the downtown area a small park contains one of the earliest of the Spanish missions dotted along the California coast. The missions were religious/military outposts of the Spanish empire, designed to consolidate Spanish rule in California by turning the indigenous population into good tax-paying Catholic citizens.

Mission San Luis Obispo de Tolosa, to give its full name, was built in 1772 and is most easy on the eye with its immaculately white stucco walls, ornate wooden doors and red-tiled roof. Mission plaza, a green space laid out around the mission building was full of Californians taking in the mild June sun. A small creek runs alongside the plaza and in an open courtyard on the far side of the creek a bar band played easy-paced reggae music ideal for a sunny afternoon. The sound floated across the creek and up the slopes of the plaza. This was congenial as it meant I could watch and listen without having to pay the bar's inflated prices.

> *A word of warning. If you're ever round this way you need to know that promenading in San Luis Obispo (SLO to the cognoscenti) on a Sunday afternoon is a serious business. This is the kind of place that people go to be seen. Wear the latest fashionable sunglasses, your best quality T-shirt and your coolest persona here or you'll run a real risk of being run out of town on a rail.*

I returned to Ventura in the early evening and found a bar to watch what turned out to be the final game of the NBA (basketball) championship series. To be honest I'm no great fan of the game (too easy to score) but this had been one of the closest championship series of recent times and I'd been pulled into the drama over the previous few weeks. The Dallas Mavericks were playing the Miami Heat. Dallas at that time was a team stuffed with canny veterans playing a team of immensely talented upstarts so naturally I was in the veterans' corner. I'd been following the Mavericks' progress from the time I'd been given a comprehensive run-down on the team's strengths, weaknesses and play-off chances by a knowledgeable fan and barfly in Port Aransas. Since then I'd sat in other bars watching their games and had begun to identify with the players, particularly the ones who might not get another shot at a title.

Not to keep you in suspense any longer, the veterans ran out champions. It was their first championship in the franchise's 31 year history, making Dallas rather than San Luis Obispo the happiest city in America, for one night at least.

SANTA MARIA
TO BAKERSFIELD

While in Ventura I'd decided that I really wanted to fit in a visit to Sequoia National Park before heading up the Pacific Coast Highway to San Francisco. The decision didn't constitute a master class in travel planning as the National Park is about 150 miles inland in eastern California. Back in the general direction I'd come from in other words. I wanted to travel to the coast for a walk through the dunes on the morning of my drive inland so my itinerary for the immediate future read:

> *Day 1; West from Santa Maria to the coast at Guadalupe, then east to Bakersfield*
>
> *Day 2; North east to Sequioa National Park then back to Bakersfield*
>
> *Day 3; Further west back to where I was on Day 1.*
>
> *Day 4; Northwards up the Pacific coast.*
>
> *– Genius!*

Still, the appeal of the whole trip had been the opportunity to travel exactly as I pleased including, it turned out, the opportunity to do things completely arse-about-face if that's what took my fancy.

The short drive west from Santa Maria to the coastal town of Guadalupe and on to the Oso Flaco State Park and the Pacific dunes is through agro-business territory. Field after field was under cultivation; broccoli, lettuce, strawberries. The fields are large and all the field workers appear to be Latinos. The signs around these outdoor factories are predominantly in Spanish.

> *Even from a distance it looked like heart-breaking work; the crops are knee-high at best and they were being tended by hand. By and large the settled population doesn't want this work. In 2010 the United Farm Workers ran a 'Take Our Jobs' campaign to entice American workers to take to the fields; 86,000 enquiries led to just 11 workers taking jobs. Farm bosses don't ask 'illegals' too many questions about papers because they work hard and they work cheap. There are three million 'illegals' in California and they've helped build the state's economy till it's now the 8th largest in the world (in the same league as Spain and Italy). Hard working 'illegals' are constantly vilified by the right-wing press and greasy politicians on the make.*

The Ranger collecting my money outside Oso Flaco State Park noticed the close attention I was paying to the notice which alerts visitors to the presence in the park of black bear, mountain lion and cougars. 'Oso Flaco' means 'skinny bear' in Spanish – the last thing I wanted to meet was any skinny (i.e. hungry) mammal bigger than I am.

When the Ranger volunteered with a smile that cougars had been spotted at the park entrance that morning I engaged her in conversation for a little while, buying time to weigh up the option of jumping back in the car. I explained that in Britain we are grateful strangers to threatening wildlife. The Ranger seemed genuinely shocked that we don't share our island with bears, bobcats or poisonous snakes. "But you have deer don't you?" she asked. I nodded in agreement but, thinking out loud, added that reports of people being mauled by deer are few and far between.

Courage summoned – after a fashion – I set off on the short walk through a small wood and along the mile-long boardwalk which crosses the dunes and the Oso Flaco Lake. Crossing the lake was the highlight of the walk. A filmy mist rose from the water, giving a mysterious feel to the place. A woman's hand rising out of the water holding a sword wouldn't have been a total surprise. Many and varied species of birds were arriving and departing every few seconds. A duck with a striking emerald blue beak (a male ruddy duck, it turned out) bobbed serenely on the ripples, unperturbed by the aerial traffic.

I was filming this watery anarchy from the boardwalk when I noticed that I had company. My new friend was on four legs and was padding confidently and inquisitively in my direction. I fought an impulse to desert the bridge for the relative safety of the water. Maybe I'd been shaken by the notice at the park entrance; in fact I was sharing the bridge with nothing more threatening than a raccoon. It came to within maybe 20 feet before its instinct for self-preservation overcame its curiosity, causing it to swerve off the boardwalk and through the guard rails. Which one of us would have finished up in the water if the raccoon had come any closer is an open question.

I followed a path through multi-coloured dune shrubbery to the Pacific. There was a mighty ocean thundering onto the beach but the coastal mist obscured everything more than 30 or 40 yards away, bringing on a strong sense of separation. A self-indulgent, not altogether unpleasant, melancholy descended, stayed for a short while, got bored with me and moved on.

The walk back to the car was notable only for the variety of paw prints in the sand dunes; most were small, some as large as a saucer and possibly cougar-paw-sized. Maybe I'd not been totally alone.

The rest of the day was taken up with the journey from the coast over the Sierras via California Route 166 to Bakersfield, my stopping-off point on the way to Sequoia National Park. Route 166 took me through neat orange groves, past a field of ugly oil derricks, over the lovely but inaccessible Twitchell Reservoir and round the edge of the Sierra Madre mountains where the temperature climbed steadily into the 90s.

The Sierras are wonderfully barren and empty. There were no gas stations, no motels, very few dwellings for about 50 miles as far as the towns of Cuyama and, even more excitingly, New Cuyama. Cuyama had 57 registered residents in the 2010 census, New Cuyama had 517. This was the America I was falling in love with. New Cuyama is situated on a small, wide plain between low-rise yellow hills. I stopped at New Cuyama's Buckhorn diner for a bite to eat. A self-mocking highway sign on the slip road leading to The Buckhorn read:

NEW CUYAMA

Population	*562*
Ft Above Sea Level	*2150*
Established	*1951*
Total	*4663*

Impeccable maths, impenetrable logic.

The Buckhorn is a cavernous fast-food joint the size of a working men's club concert room but a family of four and a couple of stray travellers were my only companions. The place had certainly seen better times. It must originally have been built to feed workers at the exhausted oil field to the south because at a push you could get all the registered residents of New Cuyama in The Buckhorn at one sitting. It could be the stage-set for a cheapskate 1970s exploitation movie, a back-of-beyond diner just begging for a gang of bikers to ride into town and terrorise the population.

I loved New Cuyama and I loved The Buckhorn and its indigestible food. It was a border town lacking a border. I'd have stayed longer except that there was nothing to see and nothing to do there. I drove away through the few fields that are under cultivation, which I imagine are all that keeps New Cuyama ticking over these days.

SEQUOIA NATIONAL PARK

I stayed in Bakersfield and was off again early the following morning, a tired and rather unhappy traveller. I'd planned a 180-mile round-trip wrapped around a hike round a National Park and it started to dawn on me that for the second day running I'd been a bit too ambitious.

The drive north through the San Joaquin valley was unremarkable, enlivened only by KZPO King's Radio Station 103.3 FM; "We've a strange selection of oldies for you today folks – it's what we like to call nostalgia." Not the usual nostalgia though – an imaginative mix of half-forgotten '40s swing, some blues, pop, '70s rock and everything in between. Lovely stuff.

In the Sequoia foothills I followed a valley road through the splendid small towns of Exeter, Lemon Cove and Three Rivers. Stopping in Exeter for refreshment I picked up a copy of the 'Kaweah Commonwealth' newspaper – "A Journal For Those Who Labor And Think" it said on the masthead. There were no factories around there so the compliment must have been aimed at Kaweah's alert independent farmers.

Further along Route 198 the Kaweah River tumbled excitedly out of the Sierra Nevada mountains and under Pumpkin Hollow Bridge near the centre of Three Rivers, last stop before the National Park. Three Rivers isn't much more than a river, a bridge and a few amenities for tourists but still it's as pretty as a picture. And clearly there was someone here with a sense of humour and/or a sense of adventure. A wooden garden chair had been placed on a prominent rock in the middle of the tumultuous, seemingly uncrossable Kaweah. Looking down from the bridge, my silent congratulations went out to the swashbuckler-comic who pulled the trick off.

The run up from the valley floor to the giant sequoia forest was beautiful but tortuous. The road wound its way up the side of a steep canyon, taking the best part of an hour. Giant sequoias grow naturally only on the western slopes of the Sierra Nevada, about a mile above sea level. Up to 3,500 years old, rust-red in colour, 250 feet high and 20 feet plus in diameter, the sequoias are stately and imperturbable natural monuments. The 'General Sherman' is the daddy, claimed to be the biggest tree in the world. An average giant sequoia, the blurb tells me, weighs more than a fully-laden jumbo jet.

Like everyone else who comes here I was keen to get a shot of myself next to one of these mighty giants but my attempts to set the camera timer and photograph myself proved fruitless – a succession of shots of my upside-down head (checking the timing mechanism) and of my receding arse (running to get in position) – until a fellow traveller took pity and got me and the sequoia into the frame together at the first time of asking.

Antelopes wandered through the sequoias at a respectable distance and, fleetingly, I spotted a young bear running through some saplings. The bear seemed panicky – briefly separated from its mother perhaps, but probably best not to be around the fretful mother to witness the reunion.

It wasn't all forest. Crescent Meadow is a pastoral idyll a mile high into the canyon; a large, flat, grassed plateau incongruously but wonderfully plonked smack dab in the middle of the sequoias. I could have been in a Kent meadow, in a parallel universe cricket could have been invented here by bored shepherds in the 18th century. I had to wander around, rather than through, Crescent Meadow though due to the pooling snowmelt and the fact that a family of bears had been spotted soaking up the sun here earlier in the day. I was desperate to see a bear in the wild but unhappy at the thought of negotiating a bend in the trail and disturbing a pissed-off one. People have died doing that.

A short bus ride across the park took me to Moro rock – an imposing granite dome rising above the surrounding countryside. The seemingly endless flights of steps to the rock's summit, over 400 of them, hacked out of the precipitous granite by FDR's Civilian Conservation Corps in the 1930s, posed a physical challenge that I almost didn't pass. A steady stream of hikers making their way up the steps ensured a degree of embarrassment for anyone turning back and helped to keep me honest.

The panorama which opened up at the summit came close to matching the Grand Canyon. A thousand feet down from the narrow, railed walkway at the peak of Moro rock a green valley floor wound its way to the Great Western Divide range of mountains on the horizon. The rock cast a dark shadow deep into the valley in the late afternoon. It was a worthy reward for the 400 steps.

I started out on the return journey much later than I'd planned but even so I was happy to halt my return journey at The Gateway Restaurant, at one end of Pumpkin Hollow Bridge, directly over the agitated Kaweah. The waitress led me to a table on the veranda, which suited me fine as the river was running directly underneath. I still harbour a suspicion that the exterior seating allocation was connected to my road-soiled appearance. No matter, the waitress was friendly – when we could make ourselves understood over the unstoppable SSSSSSSHHHH of the swollen water – and the food was more than welcome. One drink, then another and the temptation to have a few more and book in here for the night almost overcame me but I'd become a slave to my wobbly itinerary and dutifully headed off back to Bakersfield.

It turned out to be a good decision. If I'd stayed over I would have missed out on a moonlight drive past Lake Tulare and through the southern part of the San Joaquin valley. I would have missed the perfect temperature of the night air coming in through the open car windows, the full moon rising on the passenger side, the dark trees and houses slipping by and the big band music from another era playing on my car radio. Separated from the outside world by the dark emptiness of these California roads, this singularly American music had its way with me. For the length of the journey home

I was in happy communion with the country of my imagination. I should have done more long night drives when I had the chance.

BAKERSFIELD TO MORRO BAY

If Bakersfield was a boxer it would be Jake LaMotta; tough, relentless, pug-
ugly. It has a reputation as a music city. Refugees from the Depression-hit
Great Plains ensured the city would become a thriving centre for blue
collar Country music but the predominance of mining as well as oil and
natural gas production round here also ensures that Bakersfield features
somewhere near the top of the list of the most polluted cities in the US. It
was once briefly, but unhappily, known as Alkalai City.

I'd seen very little of Bakersfield, and as the drive back to the coast promised to be straightforward I decided on a little reconnaissance, mainly with a view to an early breakfast, before leaving. Unfortunately, the drive round the exotically-named Auto Mall Drive, Gasoline Alley and Motor Centre Drive didn't offer much beyond used car lots so I had to settle for eating on the road.

From Bakersfield my journey would be taking me due west to Morro Bay, maybe 150 miles or so north of Ventura, completing my long detour inland. After an hour or so I was amongst the soft greens, browns and yellows of California's coastal range again, in the Cholame Hills to be exact, easy-going rolling countryside. Cholame was a dot on the map I'd picked out in advance as my place to eat. But the town itself proved to be elusive or, as I discovered when I arrived there about an hour out of Bakersfield, non-existent.

Now I think this is fascinating so please bear with me. Cholame is what's called an 'unincorporated community' or, as the US Geographic Names Information System rather bureaucratically explains, 'A populated place that is not a census-designated or incorporated place having an official federally recognized name.' All well and good you might think, except that, at least on the day I stopped here, it's not a populated place – there's no-one living there. There's Jack's Ranch Café – and pretty nice it is too – and that's it.

It was clear when I pulled up that Jack's Ranch Café would be all business. A sign outside offers short-shrift to potential evil-doers;

TRESPASSING – JACK'S CAFÉ

"Violators will be shot. Survivors will be shot again."

Which, you might think, as a company policy could probably do with a little tidying up in the customer relations department but, on the other hand, has the virtue of being clear, concise and refreshingly to the point. Another sign pinned to a tree advised the casual visitor to beware of rattlesnakes. The uncomfortable notion began to form that the unfortunate population of Cholame had been whittled down over the years by gunfire and rattlers. But even this wouldn't explain the absence of dwellings other than the café – it all felt a little strange.

The café itself is old-time roadside Americana; net curtains, wall lights, jukebox, even some old farm machinery in the corner for decoration. And photographs - lots and lots of photographs - of James Dean. The '50s film star was killed in a car crash about a mile east of here and Jack's Ranch Café isn't about to let anyone forget it in a hurry. If you're in need of a James Dean coffee mug, pen, cigarette lighter, T-shirt or poster this place could fix you up.

> *Long story short, Dean and a passenger were speeding (literally, Dean had picked up a ticket earlier in the day) west on what is now Route 46 and had a coming together with a car, driven by a Donald Turnupseed, travelling east. Turnupseed, not noticing Dean's low-profile Porsche travelling in the opposite direction in the late afternoon sun, had tried to make a left turn across Route 46 onto Route 41 and hadn't made it. Turnupseed and Dean's passenger walked away, Dean didn't. The story goes that, having observed the formalities with the local police at the crash scene Turnupseed then hitched the 120-or-so miles back home to Tulare, which I think is an admirably composed response in the circumstances. I can't help wondering whether the driver who picked him up asked Turnupseed what sort of a day he'd had.*

There are memorial signs at the café and at the current junction of Route 46 and Route 41 but, faithful to the 'Outer Limits' nature of things around Cholame, the true crash site isn't where the sign says it is because Route 46 now follows a different path to the one it followed in 1955. Dean's fans regularly mill around in the general vicinity of the crash site on the anniversary of his death to pay homage to the actor generally credited with inventing the teenager. Without James Dean there'd probably be no 'Twilight' saga – but we shouldn't come down too hard on him for that.

Back at Jack's Ranch Café a negotiation with the waitress regarding the menu went a little awry when her pronunciation of 'tomayto' encouraged an uncharacteristic rendering by me of 'Let's Call The Whole Thing Off'. In a wavering tenor I warbled, "You say 'tomayto' and I say 'tomahto'" . The response wasn't the expected chuckle at my witticism but a genuine scowl and a turn of the heel. Next thing she was talking earnestly to another member of staff while he looked over at me with distaste, nodding slowly. A burly man occupying a bar stool who must have heard the exchange looked none-too-impressed either.

It was all a calamitous cultural misunderstanding. They may have thought I'd been mocking their accent or they may just have been offended Gershwin fans. I was sweating it either way. I could have left but I'd already ordered chilli and to have attempted an early departure may have escalated matters further. On the other hand I wondered whether retribution might involve novel additions to my chilli that I didn't want to think about too deeply. On balance sticking to my chair seemed the smart move. By the time the chilli arrived the waitress seemed to have recovered her equanimity, which of course could have been connected to her taking revenge during the preparation of my meal. Regardless, I was all smiles, tucked unhesitatingly into my food and, just to show willing, ordered a portion of apple pie (the waitress told me Jack's Ranch Café is famous for its apple pie) and left a higher-than-usual tip. International relations, I hope, had been restored.

> Checking in my rear-view mirror as I drove away I noticed a sign on the western end of the café porch matching the 'Jack's Ranch Café' sign on the eastern end. The sign read 'Cholame'. It appears that Jack's Ranch Café is Cholame and Cholame is Jack's Ranch Café. Churchill once famously described Soviet Russia as "A riddle wrapped in a mystery inside an enigma" but I bet the old warmonger never ran across this place.

On to Morro Bay, which was to be my jumping-off point for the coastal trip north to San Francisco. The bay's dual status as a tourist spot and working harbour is reflected in the two structures that visually dominate the place – Morro Rock, a volcanic plug rising out of the mouth of the harbour, and the Morro Bay Power Plant's three towering smokestacks to the north of town.

The run into town is splendid, through a lovely green valley. Over the last couple of miles it's possible to simply point the car, follow the road in the direction of the rock and take in the scenery. On first arrival the smokestacks seemed a discordant backdrop to this fishing town, out of time and out of place. They were put up by the Pacific Gas & Electric Co. in 1955 at the height of the post-war boom. It's hard to imagine they'd ever get built here now, but after just a short time these slim, smokeless 450-feet giants also had their appeal. Like the Tinsley cooling towers on the outskirts of Sheffield before they were scandalously dismantled these chimneys have become an iconic reminder of an industrial history that has passed. The power plant only runs intermittently now and is likely to be decommissioned soon, but opposition to the operation of the plant seems to centre on the harmful effects of the waste it discharges into the atmosphere and into the sea rather than the aesthetics of the smokestacks.

In the late afternoon I walked along the embarcadero, which is stuffed with seafood cafés and restaurants but still quiet this early in the season. A seal swam along the waterfront, presumably on the look-out for scraps from the boats or the eating houses. Most of the boats in the harbour are built for work rather than pleasure. One of them was being patched up, the harsh noise of an electric saw or welding equipment breaking the stillness.

Some kind of party seemed to be in full swing in one of the bars along the embarcadero. The sign outside carried the legend "For Free Trade & Sailors' Rights" suggesting it was the favoured place to stop after a long night's fishing. I was curious to find out more and paused outside, but curiosity was losing an arm-wrestling contest with the potential pitfalls involved in gatecrashing a community of drunken sailors. My nerve failed and I moved on. In the film "An American Werewolf In London" two hikers seek shelter in the "The Slaughtered Lamb", a pub on the Yorkshire moors. A hostile, threatening silence takes the place of raucous laughter as soon as the strangers enter. Convinced this will be my fate, and possibly influenced by my less than positive experience at Jack's Ranch Café, I have to report that I settled on an early night and a good book.

PACIFIC COAST
HIGHWAY

Thursday 16th June arrived, the day of my long-anticipated journey up the Pacific Coast Highway, from Morro Bay to Big Sur on US Route 1. The coast was covered by mist again, so this wouldn't be the hot, cloudless day of my imagination. Maturity had reined in a youthful appetite to take the journey in an open-top sports car. Put less gently, I had developed an age-related, Victor Meldrew-like prejudice towards people who drive open-top sports cars. The appropriate music was lined up on my iPod, however, and an early start promised a relatively open road.

And then Marcus appeared. Marcus was hitching, probably illegally the rascal, on the slip road leading to the Pacific Coast Highway. So I pulled over. The phrase I did so-and-so "as if someone else was doing it" is a terrible cliché, but as I pulled over it was as if someone else was doing it. I never thought twice about it.

When I asked Marcus where he was going I admit I was kind of hoping he was going to ask for somewhere 20 miles or so up the road. "Anywhere north" he offered, closing the door on any hint of backsliding on my part as my car was indisputably pointed north. It looked very much like Marcus would be with me for the day, which also put a dent in my plan to play my music of choice at an ear-splitting level all the way up America's west coast. My imagined journey was dissolving like so much cotton candy.

I think I know why I pulled over. A couple of weeks before I'd passed a portly, middle-aged hitcher sweating at the side of the highway. I hadn't stopped, regretted it, almost turned the car around a couple of miles further down the road but thought it would look stupid and strange to go back. I'd beaten myself up about not stopping for the next 200 miles. He had been the only hitcher I'd seen before Marcus made an appearance. A combination of heightened regulation and lurid reports of bad things happening to hitchers (and to drivers who've picked up hitchers) has almost killed off what was virtually a US national pastime up to the '60s and '70s.

So Marcus caught me on the rebound. I guessed that my new travelling companion was in his late 20s or early 30s. Short and wiry, his red hair and beard were of a piece with his intense manner. When he smiled there was a spectacular gap where an incisor tooth had gone missing. Marcus told me he lived in Tulare, around 150 miles north east of where I'd picked him up. Originally from Washington State, he was on a 3-week trip up the coast which, he hoped, would include a return trip to the beloved redwoods of his home state.

I asked him why he was on the road. "To find my god," he replied, unhesitatingly. Now if this conversation had happened before April, or almost anywhere else outside the States, it may have caused a ripple of concern. But I'd been travelling for two-and-a-half months in this priest-ridden country and had become inured to the evangelism that stalks it like an overbearing father. Besides, Marcus was wrapped up in the difficulties of his own life. He didn't seem to be on this trip to convert sinners.

Marcus may have been feeling spiritually lost but his problems were clearly rooted in this world – he confided that he'd just lost his girl and his job. I didn't press him as to why. Marcus then tells me that he feels empty most of the time and often thinks that nothing's worthwhile. He's trying to re-create a time from his past when he and his now ex-partner were in love and hitched their way up the coast. He's hoping something good will happen on the journey which will change his mood. "My maker will make it happen," he tells me. The venture smacks of desperation, a throw of the dice, but Marcus tries to be upbeat about it.

We talked a little more and watched US Route 1 unwind. A rocky outcrop tenanted by basking seals seemed like a good place to take a break. The seals are seasoned tourist attractions, posing shamelessly. Further into the day Marcus reminisced about a place overlooking the ocean where he and his lost love camped when things were right between them. He wanted to re-visit the place and thought he knew where it might be. I told him that I didn't mind taking him if he could find it. After a few false alarms Marcus pointed to a right-turn which he thought looked familiar. I drove up a steep, bumpy dirt road, but nothing looked familiar and Marcus's mood took a nosedive. He wanted to turn back, but I was the more determined of us at this point and, accompanied by Marcus's feeble protests, we ventured higher.

An excited yelp from the passenger seat brought me to a halt next to a small ledge. The ledge is just large enough to accommodate a two-person tent, a couple of small trees and a bush which doubles as a wind-break. We'd found the place where Marcus had spent the happiest days of his life. The surprise of finding it brings a moment's silence. The ledge is a good way from the highway, overlooking one of the countless promontories which punctuate the coast. The setting is just as beautifully dramatic as he had described.

The road had surrendered up views like this for mile after mile, but each bend in the highway had presented a subtle variation on the same theme, forestalling familiarity. Route 1, this precarious stripe of tarmac winding round the headlands, has burdened me with instant nostalgia. I've missed it from the day I left it behind.

There was a couple already camping on the ledge. They'd made the place quite homely by setting up an open fire and stringing a washing line between the two small trees. They were a long way from food and water up here though, so their stay would be likely to be a short one. They were understandably a little wary of the strangers who'd invaded a spot they'd chosen for its seclusion, but Marcus explained his situation and put them at their ease. We spent 10 or 15 minutes quietly taking in the scenery, talking to the couple, taking photographs and then headed on our way. Marcus was relieved that he'd found this happy place from his past and was convinced that I'd been sent by god to help him. According to Marcus we were now "road dogs" together. This is what travelling companions like us call each other.

But we had to part at my destination for the day, Big Sur, an expensive and exclusive place. I was staying at the Big Sur River Inn, a far-too-costly-for-what-it-is motel. Marcus told me he was going to wait at the side of the road for another lift, but when I looked behind he was making his way off the road and into the trees. I suspected he was going to spend the night sleeping under the stars and worried that my road dog was on the cusp. He'd told me about some things he'd done in the past that he wasn't too proud of but was adamant that he wanted to do the right thing now. He particularly wanted to be a good father to his daughter – one of the few anchors in his life – but he was seeing her much less frequently now that he'd broken up with his partner. I remember thinking that Marcus could become a bum if things didn't go the right way, and soon.

Big Sur isn't a town, it's a coastal area. Before the highway came through here (built in part by convict labour and completed with FDR's New Deal money) the harsh terrain formed by the headlands and gorges made it one of the most inaccessible spots in the country. Once the place had been tamed these same features made it the most desirable of spots. The short stretch of highway which would be my home for the night is the nearest thing that Big Sur has to a central hub, just a few log bungalows, shops, cafes and, in a nod to the hippy era, an old camper van made over as a souvenir shop.

There was still daylight left after I'd checked in and although many of Big Sur's beaches are inaccessible on foot to all but the most adventurous, I could just about make it by car to Pfieffer Beach before dark. Pfieffer Beach is two miles off the highway along a narrow, winding, unmarked road. About half-a-mile long, the sea and the shore here is generously dotted with rocks of all sizes. Arches have been worn in some of the larger rocks out to sea and the ocean funnels noisily through them. I'd arrived at a good time, the sun was bright and low and the tide was coming in fast and agitated, impatient to get to the shore. A walk along the beach was a bit of a chicken run; stay too close to home and you'd miss all the fun, go too far and the tide could cut off your retreat. There were just a handful of us on the beach and we were all making the same calculation. Without speaking we acknowledged with glances and smiles the brief, shared excitement of an adventure that threatened no genuine danger beyond a slight soaking.

On the day that had lived in my imagination for at least 40 years the only thing that had gone as I'd imagined it was that I'd successfully transported myself up the Pacific Coast Highway in one piece. It had been memorable nonetheless; if John Lennon is right and life is what happens while you're busy making other plans I'd lived a full life on this day at least.

SALINAS, MONTEREY & SANTA CRUZ

The day after my stroll on Pfieffer Beach I took a walk to Pfieffer Falls, which is on the Pfieffer Trail in the Pfieffer Big Sur State Park, not to be confused with the Julia Pfieffer Burns State Park which is a few miles north. A Big Sur pioneer family, the Pfieffers are very big around here.

I had to backtrack a few miles down the highway to find the entrance to the State Park and saw Marcus hitching at the side of the road again. As suspected he'd spent the night in the woods. We chatted and I promised to take him a little further up the road if he hadn't picked up a lift by the time my walk was finished. In the gloom that had settled for days over the coastal strip the trek along the Valley View trail was unremarkable, though the sight of the California morning mist rolling in quickly and thickly over the tops of low peaks held a claustrophobic appeal.

When I pointed the car northwards again a couple of hours later Marcus was still at the side of the road. I couldn't get him much further today but couldn't abandon him either so temporarily we were road dogs again. Marcus had slept next to a stream running through the woods; it had been a damp night but his sleeping bag is a good one he told me, so no complaints. We travelled together another 30 miles to Point Lobos State Reserve, whose stretch of coast I wanted to explore. I dropped Marcus at the entrance to Point Lobos with the same promise to take him a little further if his hitching thumb hadn't done the trick by the time I returned. Two hours later and Marcus was gone (or retreated to the woods again). On this short second journey I'd found out that he was much older than I'd guessed, going on 40, so his is a genuine mid-life crisis.

Point Lobos is a rocky headland of granite and sandstone, a good place for whale watching at certain times of the year. The walk was peaceful, undramatic. Rock pools, quiet coves, interesting seaweed, driftwood and the Pacific. Point Lobos probably deserved more attention but I was due in Watsonville by late afternoon that day.

I'd arranged to stay with Mary in Watsonville for a few days. An adult education tutor who on the side played percussion in a Brazilian band, Mary proved to be an interesting person to spend time with. I'd picked out Watsonville as a good place to stay because it was in striking distance of Salinas, Monterey and Santa Cruz, the main places in the Monterey Bay area that I wanted to visit.

The first person to greet me at Mary's house, though, was Mike. His familiar manner led me to conclude that he must be Mary's house partner, but it turned out he was just there to fix the sink. Before I'd had time to fish my suitcase out of the car

Mike had revealed that he'd been married three times and that his current romantic interest was, as he put it, busting his ass to become Mrs Mike No. 4. It was heady stuff for a first meeting.

This wasn't the first time since arriving in the States that a near-stranger had practically told me their life story. The openness of Americans can be an attractive quality in combination with some curiosity regarding the other person in the conversation. Unfortunately, this didn't apply to Mike. I learned that he was doing a course on the writings of Steinbeck (most praiseworthy) and that he knows exactly where my home town of Sheffield is located (most unusual). Mike also passed on a welter of information about Mary's drainage difficulties that I didn't strictly need to know, possibly breaching the plumbers' confidentiality code, but asked me nothing about myself. As a lone traveller devoting three months of his life to discovering the land of Mike's birth I thought I might warrant at least a couple of questions, out of courtesy if nothing else, but Mike talked up a storm then left.

Mary proved to be a good talker and a good listener. We had quite a few things in common; she worked in adult education as I had before my retirement, she was a shop steward and I'd been a union rep for many years, we both had grandchildren and shared a love of music. Mary told me that she'd been married but was now separated. During her marriage she'd worked at Safeways supermarket, a "union job, decent pay" as Mary put it, and she'd been reasonably comfortable, if unfulfilled. When her marriage had broken up she'd improved her qualifications and picked up a few extra hours teaching at the local Adult Education College. She found she enjoyed the teaching so much she gave up the supermarket job to teach full-time. A difficult choice as, with overtime, Mary could earn as much or more in Safeways as she could as a teacher. Mary teaches English, mainly to Mexican immigrants but increasingly to Afghan and Iraqi newcomers, in the country as a result of the US's military adventures over the past 20 years.

Just as subjects of the British empire gravitated to the empire's centre, so the US empire seems to suck in a proportion of those it goes to war with. Mexicans, Japanese, Koreans, Vietnamese have been joined now by the displaced from 9/11's aftermath. Another sign that the occupations of Iraq and Afghanistan are failing, collaborators have had to flee to the US in fear of their lives. A reverse occupation in miniature.

The right to education is under attack in America, jobs are being lost in the college Mary works in and she was pessimistic about the chances of a fightback. The union was looking for a deal to stop compulsory redundancies, there was no talk of strike action. Mary was trying to stay one step ahead by studying for a Masters degree in online teaching just in case her job went belly-up. In the absence of a wider fightback this is how it is for most Americans at the moment (most Europeans too for that matter); sink or swim, do whatever it takes to keep your head above water. We parted just before midnight, all talked out. Mary warned me that she often works on her M.A. through the night and apologised in advance in case the noise disturbed me.

At 9.30 in the morning, I padded into the kitchen, yawning, and found Mary fast asleep at the kitchen table. And I mean asleep. She was slumped in her chair, head thrown back, arms pointing to the floor, mouth wide open, snoring. Her nocturnal studying had caught up with her, the laptop on the kitchen table was powered up but unattended. Mary would have a sore neck when she eventually woke up but interrupting her sleep didn't seem the right thing to do.

> *As a youngster I'd gobbled up twentieth century American novels, none more so than the novels of John Steinbeck and today I was visiting Salinas and the Steinbeck National Centre. Steinbeck was born and raised in Salinas and set many of his books in the Monterey Bay area.*

> *From first acquaintance I'd been hooked by the straightforward realism of Steinbeck's Depression-era novels. In his biography, Jay Parini writes about the "almost childlike simplicity" of Steinbeck's prose, a deceptive simplicity that had academics and literary critics getting all sniffy at the popularity of his work. For myself, I can still remember the lump in my throat when George put an end to Lennie's troubled life in 'Of Mice And Men', 'Grapes Of Wrath' made me angry and turned my thoughts to socialism, the down-at-heel inhabitants of 'Tortilla Flat' and 'Cannery Row' burst with life while 'Travels With Charley' had awakened the idea of exploring America. A New Deal Democrat, Steinbeck's novels burnt with rage at the cruelties of 1930s America at the same time as they celebrated the irrepressibility of those struggling at the bottom of the pile.*

I'd been warned by Mary that Salinas wasn't much of a place to look at, but in fact I found much to admire in its small downtown area. The splendid frontages of the Maya and Fox Theatres, the iconic blue sign of the Greyhound bus station (sitting on top of an admittedly featureless building), the small but busy flea market on Main Street.

I took lunch in Sang's Restaurant ("Where John Steinbeck Ate!" according to a sign outside the eating house) and moved on to the National Steinbeck Centre next door. The centre is organised around his major works, with separate exhibits for each book, audio presentations and short clips of films based on Steinbecks' novels. The centrepiece is Rocinante, the pick-up camper in which Steinbeck undertook the tour of America that he wrote about in 'Travels with Charley'. It's a gorgeous thing, a cream single-berth caravan mounted on a green General Motors pick-up. Restored and presented to the Centre in 1998 the camper van is worth the price of admission on its own. Steinbeck named the camper after Don Quixote's mount, Rocinante, to emphasise the quixotic nature of his trip. It's wonderfully primitive compared to some of the behemoths ploughing up and down America's roads today and while some people doubt that Steinbeck actually covered all the ten thousand miles that he claimed in his book, what I wouldn't have given just to drive down to Monterey, my next stop, and spend a night in Rocinante.

The bay at Monterey is just about perfect but the main harbour road, Cannery Row (named by the city fathers in 1958 in honour of their local-boy-made-good), has all the form and none of the substance of the place that inspired Steinbeck. Monterey was a major industrial fishing port for decades but over-fishing led to a collapse in the industry in the 1950s. If you squeeze your eyes together and look down Cannery Row you can imagine that it's still the working port it once was. Elevated, enclosed walkways spanning the road are still emblazoned with insignias from this bygone era; MONTEREY CANNING CO., CANNERY ROW COMPANY. But the old harbour buildings now house souvenir shops, boutiques and bistros. The Monterey Canning Co. and the Cannery Row Company are shopping centres. A poster trading on Steinbeck's name stands next to the Monterey Plaza Hotel's Human Resource Office. Monterey's waterfront is a seductive, elegant fraud.

On Saturday night I spotted something in Santa Cruz that might be worthwhile. I made my way down to Moe's Alley to see The Mother Hips, a band whose name had drifted past me from time to time on internet music trawls. Moe's Alley has what people round here like to call a 'good vibe'. A small music venue just off the Cabrillo Highway to the north of Santa Cruz, Moe's attracts the cream of the almost-famous to its stage. It's a terrific venue, very intimate – exposed roofbeams, wrap-around viewing area, a quiet eating room serving good food round the back.

The Mother Hips fit the venue well; young(ish) long-hairs extemporising solos over mainstream rock riffs. 'Jam-rock' is the unfortunate catch-all for this type of stuff, The Grateful Dead and The Allman Brothers Band provide the template. I'm a bit of a sucker for dual lead guitars and the Hips' guitarists worked up a fine head of steam together, Scott Thunes' intricate bass runs keeping the whole thing ticking along nicely. My attention kept being drawn back to the drummer whose faithfully retro look, Zapata moustache and all, put me in mind of Bobby Robson's Ipswich team.

Sunday brought a bit of a shock. When I opened the curtains the California coast offered me a practically cloudless sky for the first time. As this was the northern California coast it was far from burning hot. Santa Cruz town today, a 14/15 mile journey to the opposite end of Monterey Bay. My notebook for downtown Santa Cruz records my immediate impressions; "eco, veggie, New Age, friendly, trendy shops".

The Santa Cruz boardwalk was different again. It hosts big rides, mini-golf, a 19th century carousel, arcades, ice cream vendors, test-your-strength, knock-down skittles and a shooting range. A country fair by the sea. On the beach organised girls' and boys' junior football games were under way. It looks like a beach football league; there are referees, nets, proper marked-out pitches and anxious-looking parents. Black, white and Latino working class families were out for the day. Tattoos, muffin tops, fast food, running arguments with the kids. A brilliant, vibrant place. I outstayed my time there and left with regret – San Francisco, my final destination of the trip, awaited me the next day.

SAN FRANCISCO & HOME

San Francisco is every bit as overwhelming as New York. But it overwhelms in a more self-conscious, less nose-to-nose sort of way. There was a pleasing symmetry to the trip in that I spent most of my first day there people-watching in San Francisco's Union Square, just as I had spent my first full day in New York's Union Square. The West Coast version of the square is populated by hustlers, buskers, gawpers, workers, slackers, compulsive shoppers and the conspicuously and flamboyantly mentally ill. All were, in turn, both the audience and the show.

"The coldest winter I ever spent was a summer in San Francisco," may be the wittiest thing Mark Twain never wrote and a gross libel on the city's micro-climate, but even in late June it's best to pay close attention to what's happening overhead. Fog clouds can race in from the Pacific, overwhelm a perfectly blue sky and turn summer into late autumn in a matter of minutes. This was exactly how the weather was shaping up when I undertook a chill, blustery open-top bus tour to the Golden Gate Bridge. So you can imagine our tour party's surprise when we came across a couple of hardy pedestrians on Market Street, middle-aged, respectable and completely naked except for hats and shoes.

My admiration for these baby boomers, who had shrugged off all inhibitions to stroll and smile amongst open-mouthed shoppers, was unbounded. Our tour double-decker almost tipped over as the entire party pushed over to the same side of the bus to get photographs of the happy couple. A city ordinance has since made this sort of exhibitionism illegal, which is a real shame. This city played a prominent role in the invention of those consummate show-offs, beatniks and hippies; the term 'beatnik' was first coined in the San Francisco press and if you wanted to wear flowers in your hair you made a bee-line here. How much duller would life be without show-offs?

The first thing you notice as you approach the Golden Gate Bridge is that it isn't the least bit golden but an eye-catching orangey-red. The 'Golden Gate' refers not to the bridge itself but the headlands that it connects – San Francisco peninsula to the south, Marin peninsula to the north.

The second thing you notice is that it's an architectural wonder to match the natural wonders of the Grand Canyon and Monument Valley. Slim and sleek, gracefully arched over a deep, treacherous stretch of water, it's not until you're almost on top of the bridge that you take in the scale of the thing. A six-lane highway runs down the centre of the bridge, with room for a pedestrian and cycle walkway either side. The tops of the stately north and south towers holding the bridge's suspension wires are over 200 metres above the water, disappearing into the clouds when the fog rolls in.

I was reminded of the sombre thoughts provoked by the Grand Canyon. The grandeur of the canyon had occasioned a meditation on flying and dying. Over the years the beauty of the bridge has tempted a shockingly large number of desperate people (more than a thousand since the bridge was built in 1937) to act on their darkest thoughts and finish themselves off here. In 2011, 37 climbed over the low safety rail and threw themselves into the void. A further hundred people were prevented from jumping, so on average in 2011 someone jumped or attempted to jump from this elegant tourist trap every two-and-a-half-days. The number of jumpers peaks about 18 months after the onset of economic recession, round about the period when unemployment benefit starts to run out for the newly jobless.

Most people jump from the side of the bridge that takes in views of the city and San Francisco Bay; aesthetics on the verge of oblivion.

There are things that could be done. Many of the world's leading tourist spots (the Eiffel Tower for instance) have installed safety nets. A few years ago, the cost of a safety net for the bridge was estimated at around $45 million, roughly the combined annual salaries of the top 4 professional basketball players with the Golden Gate Warriors. But while there's big money in professional sports there's no money in saving lives and the net hasn't been built yet. The cheaper option is to install crisis counselling telephones; there are eleven of them on the pedestrian walkways to help save less determined jumpers.

More symmetry to end the journey; a ticket to watch the San Francisco Giants baseball team play the Minnesota Twins, the same team I'd watched the Yankees breeze past in New York. I took a cable-car (on the running board, heart pounding) from downtown to Fisherman's Wharf then strolled a scenic mile or so by the bay to the Giants' AT&T ball park.

The little cable-cars that climb halfway to the stars are every bit as much fun as you'd imagine and it turns out the drivers are comedy gold when it comes to abusing the passengers:

"Fisherman's Wharf, end of the line, now get off and do something else."

"Please stay inside the car, my first day on the job and I do not want to have to do the paperwork if you die."

"Please do not lean out of the car, the theory of natural selection applies here."

And so on.

The combination of these frail-looking vehicles and San Francisco's harsh topography is one of the city's most celebrated features. There are so many hills here that even local experts don't seem able to agree on a number. The original Nob Hill is in San Francisco, its elevation has guaranteed exclusivity for the rich since the late

19th century. But even on rarified Nob Hill the city fathers made no allowance for the hilly terrain when they laid out the street grid, driving the streets straight and steep up the hillsides, creating a new panorama on every corner.

AT&T Park looked a picture on the sunny Thursday afternoon that I watched the Giants beat the Minnesota Twins. The bleachers were awash with Giants' orange, in dazzling contrast with the vivid green and sandy brown of the playing area. The fans here are loud and enthusiastic but lack the dismissive wit of the New Yorkers.

The home team were fielding their explosive pitcher, Tim Lincecum. Young and rangy, Lincecum looked as if he was fresh out of the woods but he was a rising force in the game and his speed and accuracy kept the Twins' bats quiet all afternoon. In 2011 the Giants had, in Brian Wilson, probably the second-best closing pitcher in the major leagues behind the Yankees' Mariano Rivera. Wilson is a fearsome-looking opponent, 6'2, over 15 stones, chest-length, jet-black beard, mohawk haircut. And he can pitch at 100mph plus. Though the Giants' batters didn't fire on the day, Lincecum and Wilson were good enough to take care of the Twins without much help. Twins 1, Giants 2.

Joe was my host for the last five days of the trip. A friend of a friend, I'd emailed him a few months before making the trip and he'd agreed to put me up for the duration of my stay in San Francisco. Ignoring my protests, he'd moved me into his bedroom while he slept in the spare bedroom next to the downstairs garage.

Joe is a gay ex-military officer who saw active service in Vietnam but, increasingly aware that his sexual preferences didn't sit well with the military approach to life, he took an early pension and immersed himself in San Francisco's gay community. An active volunteer for years in HIV/AIDS-related charities and in the early days of San Francisco's Gay Pride festival, Joe admits that he's starting to slow down and supports his causes with money rather than time these days.

Joe is quiet, interesting, serious, occasionally morose and considerate to a fault. I'd been warned that our politics might clash but we had long discussions over dinner on a couple of evenings and over lunch on a day trip to the delightfully-named Half Moon Bay, and whilst American foreign policy proved a bone of contention, the discussion never reached boiling point. Joe adhered to some fairly commonplace racial stereotypes (Mexicans are mostly lazy, Asians work hard and look after their own, black neighbourhoods are trouble) but he carried his prejudices lightly. We agreed to disagree.

A slightly awkward moment when Joe first showed me around his bedroom: one entire wall is covered with scores of artfully posed naked photographs of friends and lovers. An astonishing and impressive array of bums, cocks and beards. What to say? I chose silence. For Joe the photos must have become commonplace over the years so he didn't feel the need to comment either. As a result we let this elephant in the room wander around bellowing and destroying the furniture while we made small talk. My timidity was undone a couple of days later. For the life of me I hadn't been able to locate the switch for the big light in Joe's bedroom. With his guidance I discovered that the switch had been cleverly located in the middle of the photographs. One knob that I had overlooked. At that point we were able to usher the elephant out of the room and discuss the lives and the stories behind Joe's photographs.

On my last night out in the States I went to see Terry Evans at the Biscuits & Blues Club on Mason Street. Terry Evans was one of Ry Cooder's backing singers in the 1970s and '80s and a member of possibly the most accomplished of Ry Cooder's line-ups (and therefore one of the most accomplished rock bands to have graced a stage), the fabulously named Moula Banda Rhythm Aces. Evans cut albums with fellow Rhythm Ace Bobby King as well as a number of sadly neglected soul and gospel-influenced solo albums that are still worth hunting down. Musical fame is passing, though, and tonight Terry is doing the early show, singing straight-down-the-line blues with a small band to a half-empty club. His warm, strong tenor is still well in evidence though, the band is enthusiastic and on top of their jobs and the sparse crowd warmed up after a couple of beers.

I'd have loved to have told Terry Evans at the end of the show that I was 5,000 miles from home, had been appreciating his music for going on 40 years and had got a massive kick from seeing him perform so close up. But he was monopolised by fans wanting endless selfies with the star of the show, so I walked out into the night humming his songs and thinking of home.

On my final day I toured the Haight-Ashbury district, possibly the best-known neighbourhood in the States in the '60s. It had seen better days but is still able to trade off memories of its heyday; The Pipe Dream Store, The Cannabis Company, the Anarchist Collective Bookstore, Jimi Hendrix posters everywhere you go. I arrived early in the morning, the best time of day to appreciate Haight-Ashbury, and had the best coffee and bagel of the trip listening to psychedelic-era Beatles.

Stretching from the end of Haight Street to the western edge of the San Francisco peninsula is Golden Gate Park and the whole of my last afternoon was spent walking through its grounds to the de Young Museum of Fine Art.

I stayed a while at the National Aids Memorial Grove, an area of the park made over to the memory of the thousands who died of the illness. The memorial pays tribute in particular to the grassroots movement that gave birth to the 'San Francisco Model' of AIDS treatment, based on compassionate nursing, palliative care, multi-agency working and health education. This may sound like nothing more than common sense these days, but in the early '80s when the 'mystery gay epidemic' hit San Francisco during the icy years of Reaganism, this was a path-breaking approach that had to be fought for hard and that the city is rightly proud of.

There was a Picasso Exhibition on at the de Young Museum with over a hundred pieces from the Musée National Picasso in Paris, borrowed while the Musée was shut for renovation. I paid a bit extra to take the audio tour and, I think, came out significantly less ignorant than I'd gone in. The short version is that Picasso turned out work in many different mediums, including the use of found objects; eccentricities of form in his paintings and drawings stemmed from an urge to portray a 3-dimensional world using a 2-dimensional medium; his work regularly referenced the old masters and also reflected his radicalism, sexism, playfulness and love of Spain. A treat for the soul and I could have gone around twice if my legs hadn't given out.

And, just like that, I was out of there. No rousing climax to the story, no great revelatory episode to put my journey into a neat contextual framework. When is life ever like that outside the movies? There was a final dinner date with Joe, a few (fully clothed) photos as mementos, a final piece of American hospitality – a lift to the airport – handshakes, hugs, some manly misting and off into the sky. I was ready for home to tell the truth, I'd been a long time away and, to pinch a line from Woody Guthrie, I was tired of being a stranger.

A FEW AFTERTHOUGHTS
& LOOSE ENDS

US history crossed Carol and my paths in while we were in New Orleans. Barack Obama announced that US forces had tracked down and killed Osama bin Laden in Pakistan. As you can imagine, the news was a very big deal around the breakfast tables in the hotel we were staying in. The contented smiles of our fellow guests were reflected on millions of American faces. I can still recall the TV images of crew-cut, button-down college kids waving the stars and stripes in celebration and their guttural 'U-S-A' chanting. Years later every detail of Obama's announcement - except the fact that bin Laden was dead - has been challenged. The investigative journalist Seymour Hirsh contends that bin Laden's hide-out wasn't discovered by systematic, painstaking CIA sleuthing or by successful water-boarding as Obama claimed but by a 'walk-in' informant; the perpetrator of 9/11 wasn't tracked down to a 'Dr Evil'-style command and control centre armed to the teeth but was a prisoner of the ISI, Pakistan's secret service, held in a compound under their control. The US did a deal with the ISI; when the Navy SEAL team flew in, bin Laden's guards walked out. There was no firefight, just a shooting.

Bin Laden's assassination helped Obama to reclaim the Presidency of the United States in 2012 but the processes of history can thwart even the most powerful person on earth. Bin Laden's organisation didn't collapse on cue when he was taken out of the picture. In fact, at the time he was killed bin Laden had effectively been sidelined from the al-Qaeda leadership. The fury of people across the Middle East, suffering under American occupation and the dictatorship of western-backed tyrants for years, fed into support for the even more violent sectarianism of ISIS. Despite the trillion dollars spent on the 'war on terrorism', at the time of writing large swathes of Syria, Iraq and Yemen are contested by America's sworn enemies. This doesn't look like victory for the US, but it is a continuing nightmare for the people of the Middle East.

The fading Obama stickers in New York, the memorials to the martyrs of the civil rights struggle in the Deep South and my afternoon with Annie Pearl Avery are brought back into focus by the continuing war waged on black men by racist cops throughout 2014 and 2015. Whatever the gains made by the struggle to win civil rights for African-Americans in the 1960s, the apparent impunity with which white cops can shoot, suffocate and beat blacks shows the need for a continuation of that struggle. The last time I checked Annie Pearl was still going strong and had been arrested in the Alabama State Capitol building while protesting in support of the extension of medical aid for low-income families (she and her co-defendants were found not guilty) and had recorded an interview for the US Library Of Congress about her involvement in the civil rights movements. The Black Lives Matter and other civil rights campaigns will need many fighters cast in Annie Pearl's mould.

The Sterick and Sears Crosstown buildings in Memphis still stand empty. Complications arising from the separate ownership of building and land dictate that the 29-storey Sterick, a building once known as the 'Queen of Memphis' is unlikely to be renovated before the 99-year lease on the land runs out on 30th April 2025. Memphis's 2,000 homeless may feel that it could be put to some use before then, but the brutal realities of the real estate market dictate that commercially, if not socially, the Sterick is currently worthless.

Four years further on, the authorities running the Golden Gate Bridge have finally agreed on a final design and funding of $76 million for a suicide barrier at the span. The barrier isn't expected to be completed before 2019. Discussion of a barrier first began in the 1950s and on average two dozen people jump from the bridge each year so the cost in human lives of the 60-year delay is still mounting.

This is how things move on; continuity and change. A great writer once speculated that historical events repeat themselves first as tragedy, then as farce. The election of Donald Trump to the presidency of the United States just days before I sat down to write these words suggests that sometimes tragedy and farce can manifest themselves in the same event.

First things first. Trump's election is a disaster for everyone who wants to see progressive change in America. The Ku Klux Klan grand wizard endorsed Trump's candidacy. Fascists from the National Policy Institute, meeting in Washington D.C. just days after Trump's victory, certainly felt their time had arrived. 'Hail Trump!' they chanted. 'Hail victory!' replied the speaker which, in the original German, translates as 'Seig Heil'. Every racist bum in America will have been emboldened by Trump's victory and his cabinet appointments leave little doubt about the reactionary policies he will be pursuing.

That Americans can vote a misogynist, racist snake-oil salesman like Trump into the most powerful office in the US will have confirmed for many on this side of the Atlantic that the US is beyond redemption. The lazy stereotype of the ignorant, overweight blue-collar American will persist, maybe even strengthen.

But the same white working class voters in the key 'Rust Belt' states who didn't trust Clinton in 2016 also voted in America's first black president in 2008 and 2012. In Michigan, Wisconsin and Pennsylvania the Democratic vote dropped by between 13 and 9 percentage points compared to Obama's performance in 2012. Clinton's problem was that Obama hadn't delivered in his 8 years and she was the living embodiment of a US establishment which had enriched itself while presiding over the loss of 5 million industrial jobs. People in the rust belt and beyond felt their lives and their futures were being destroyed and didn't like it one bit.

In many parts of the country low-paid service jobs had replaced well-paid union jobs - does this sound familiar? People felt they were working harder for less -

and they were right. In 2016 real wages for those at the sharp end of the economy were, on average, below what they had been 40 years before; people in full-time employment were reporting an average working week of 47 hours with just 15 days a year paid holiday compared to a European average of 28 days. I met and talked to these people in 2011; taxi drivers, nurses, college lecturers, bartenders. American workers were hurting when the 2016 election came round and they were ready to bust somebody in the nose. Billionaire Trump was able to insinuate himself into this situation as an establishment 'outsider' and to hitch people's legitimate concerns to the most reactionary of impulses by pinning the blame on Latinos, Muslims and immigrants.

It didn't have to be this way. Before the party high-ups shut down his campaign Bernie Sanders, standing openly as a 'democratic socialist', had won an impressive 13 million votes in the Democratic primary elections and performed strongly in states like Ohio, Wisconsin and Michigan which eventually turned the election for Trump. Sanders had channelled the vitriol where it belonged; towards Wall Street whose greed led to financial disaster and recession, and towards the tax-dodging 1% at the top of the heap who have hoovered up over 40% of the nation's wealth. The Democratic Party establishment took fright at Bernie's anti-establishment message, gagged it, and in doing so sentenced itself to 4 years of impotence.

So Trump won by default; only a quarter of those entitled to vote supported him. He lost the popular ballot by over 2 million votes but won in the Electoral College - a quaint US institution dreamed up by the founding fathers in the 18th century to protect the interests of slaveholding states. Trump won chiefly because support for Clinton fell through the floor - she lost 6.5 million votes compared to Obama's victory in 2008 - not because of an overwhelming endorsement of Trump's views.

This is important because it means Trump has a weak mandate. There have been promising signs of a fightback already; from Portland to New York, Denver to Baltimore thousands came out to protest Trump's victory. As I write, environmental campaigners and supporters of Native American rights are celebrating a famous victory in stopping an oil pipeline planned to run near to the Sioux reservation at Standing Rock, North Dakota. The fight being waged by fast food workers for a minimum wage of $15 and the right to belong to a union is taking off and inspiring low-paid workers in Britain to raise their own campaign. This is the America I recognise and experienced when I met with the small but determined group of socialists in Austin, the baby-boomer radicals of Arizona, the union rep fighting redundancies in Watsonville.

America has a long and honourable history of radicalism which at times like these seems to be buried under a dominant salute-the-flag-and-kick-some-ass chauvinism. But the great union strikes of the early 20th century and the 1930s, the civil rights and anti-war campaigns of the 1960s and the liberation movements against gay and women's oppression won't be written out of history and are waiting to be reclaimed by a new generation of fighters.

POSTCRIPT

America is no longer an abstraction to me now, light and shadows on a screen. It's made of the same stuff as the rest of the planet, just moulded on a vastly larger scale, giving a misleading sense of permanence. The Colorado river still cuts into the Grand Canyon, changing it minutely every day over vast tracts of time. Human activity creates change on a more human timescale; deserts expand, forests recede, new ghost towns are thrown up by de-industrialisation. In 2011 I knew these places as they were then because I saw them, walked them, smelled them, enveloped myself in them. I cling to the thought that I might do it all again one of these days.

"I shall be telling this with a sigh
Somewhere ages and ages hence:
Two roads diverged in a wood, and I,
I took the one less traveled by,
And that has made all the difference."

Robert Frost

Made in the USA
Columbia, SC
19 October 2017